General Editors: Professor A.N. Jeffares (*University of Stirling*) & Professor Suheil Bushrui (*American University of Beirut*)

William Golding

THE SPIRE

Notes by Hilda D. Spear

MA (LONDON) PH D (LEICESTER) FIBA
Lecturer in English, University of Dundee

LONGMAN
YORK PRESS

ACKNOWLEDGEMENTS

I should like to thank for help in various ways: Miss Diane Fray, The Reverend Jonathan Eades, Mr Abdel-Moneim Aly and the staff of Dundee University Library. Thanks are also due to Mrs Moira Anthony and my daughter Kathryn for assistance with typing.

H.D.S.

YORK PRESS
Immeuble Esseily, Place Riad Solh, Beirut.

LONGMAN GROUP LIMITED
Longman House,
Burnt Mill,
Harlow,
Essex

© Librairie du Liban 1985

First published 1985
ISBN 0 582 79297 5
Produced by Longman Group (FE) Ltd
Printed in Hong Kong

Contents

Part 1

Introduction

THOUGH HE DESCRIBES HIMSELF as a Wiltshireman, William Golding was born in Cornwall, on 19 September 1911. He has, however, lived in Wiltshire for most of his life. He remembers walking on the Marlborough Downs as a boy of fourteen, and wanting 'to go back to Cornwall and the sea'; it was a moment of rare disloyalty to Wiltshire for, like the poet Charles Sorley before him, Golding became infatuated with the 'particularly ancient and mysterious history that has left its mark in every corner' of Wiltshire.

His formal education began at the age of six in one of those small private elementary schools known as 'Dame Schools' because they were run by a woman, generally an elderly spinster, or a widow. Side by side with his school education was the less formal education which he gained through outings with his mother, such as that to the British Museum when he was seven years old. There the fascination of the great Egyptian collection captured his imagination. (It was not until many years later, in 1976, that he fulfilled a lifetime's ambition by visiting Egypt.) After the Dame School Golding attended Marlborough Grammar School where his abiding love of Greek language and literature began. When he left school he went to Brasenose College, Oxford, where he read for his B.A. degree. In 1966, by which time he was already an established novelist, he was honoured by being elected an Honorary Fellow of Brasenose College.

In 1934 Golding's first book, *Poems*, was published by Macmillan. For twenty years it looked as though it would be his only publication. He married Ann Brookfield in 1939 and that same year he began teaching at Bishop Wordsworth's School which is situated in the Close of Salisbury Cathedral. It was the year the Second World War broke out. The following year, at the age of twenty-nine, Golding joined the Royal Navy. He remained on active service throughout the war, returning home in 1945. He then resumed his job as schoolmaster at Bishop Wordsworth's School and continued teaching until 1961.

During the latter part of this time he began to find himself creatively. By now he was a family man with a son, David, and a daughter, Judith. He had also established himself as a novelist. In the essay 'A Moving Target' from the book of that name (1982) he records that as a boy of thirteen he began his first novel; he never progressed beyond the first sentence. He continued, however, to write; sometimes he made plans for books; sometimes he wrote odd sentences; three times he wrote whole novels and sent them off to publishers only to have them rejected. He tells us that at that time he had not found his own voice; all he was doing was imitating or parodying the work of earlier writers. He then decided that as other people did not seem to want to read his novels he might just as well write to please himself. The impetus came to him as he read bedtime stories to his two children. As a reaction to the romantic adventure stories 'with their paper cutout goodies and baddies and everything for the best in the best of all possible worlds' (*A Moving Target*, p.163) he decided to write a realistic story about boys on an island and to show how they really would behave. The book was *Lord of the Flies* and it was published in 1954 by Faber; it was an immediate success. It has been reprinted numerous times both in Britain and in the United States, and has been turned into a film. Moreover, it has become a popular 'set book' for examinations in schools.

It was all but twenty years since the publication of *Poems*. Golding was now almost forty-three and suddenly the channels of his creative energy were opened up. *Lord of the Flies* was followed by *The Inheritors* in 1955 and by *Pincher Martin* in 1956. By 1961, when he gave up teaching, Golding had published a book of poems, four novels, a play and the short story, 'Envoy Extraordinary' (1956); he had also become book reviewer for *The Spectator*. During the year 1961–2 he went to the United States of America where he was Visiting Professor at Hollins College, Virginia. After that he devoted himself to writing. *The Spire* was published in 1964, his first collection of non-fictional pieces, *The Hot Gates*, in 1965, *The Pyramid* in 1967 and *The Scorpion God* in 1971. Then it looked for a while as though his source of inspiration had dried up. By the late nineteen-seventies postgraduate students were boldly writing dissertations on him, confident in the belief that he would produce no more novels. Fortunately they were wrong, for 1979 saw the publication of a new novel, *Darkness Visible*, swiftly followed in 1980 by *Rites of Passage* and in 1984 by *The Paper Men*. Additionally, his second collection of non-fictional pieces, *A Moving Target* was published in 1982. Golding, indeed, remains a moving target and readers of these Notes or of any other book on him should be alert to the fact that every new novel he publishes may slightly alter our view of his work as a whole.

When Golding was a small boy he travelled in his imagination; in the last twenty years he has become a seasoned traveller in reality. He has travelled to many countries in Europe, to America and to Egypt; yet most of his novels appear to owe little in any direct way to these travels. Nevertheless, in every book he writes he is reflecting the world as he sees it and his varied experiences contribute to the kaleidoscopic vision of his novels.

Golding's contribution to literature has been recognised not only through the publication of his novels and through the many critical books and articles on him (a bibliography published in the *Bulletin of Bibliography* in 1979 lists no fewer than one hundred and seventy-one critical pieces on his work by that time, excluding reviews), but also by certain honours accorded him. In 1955 he was elected to a Fellowship of the Royal Society of Literature. In 1966, the year that he was made an honorary Fellow of Brasenose College, he was awarded a C.B.E. and in 1970 the University of Sussex gave him an Honorary D.Litt. degree. His two novels *Darkness Visible* and *Rites of Passage* were awarded respectively the James Tait Black Memorial Prize and the Booker McConnell Prize. Then, in 1983, the most prestigious of all literary awards, the Nobel Prize for Literature, was bestowed on him.

Golding was born three years before the outbreak of the Great War; he was born into an era of leisured tranquillity which passed away with the war and has never been seen since. The terrible horrors and physical violence of the First World War were followed by the miseries, in Britain at least, of the Depression. The nineteen-thirties brought the disillusionment of the Spanish Civil War. From the age of three, Golding has never lived in a world at peace. It is perhaps not surprising that he does not see progress and civilisation as improving forces.

His first novel, *Lord of the Flies* (1954), takes war as its starting point. The boys he depicts are escaping from the adult madness of armed conflict and genocide. Civilisation has not taught them to survive happily in primitive surroundings. What they seem to have learnt is war and the art of war, hostility, the 'power game'. We may be reminded of Wilfred Owen's poem 'A Terre':

> I suppose
> Little I'd ever teach a son, but hitting,
> Shooting, war, hunting, all the arts of hurting.

Lord of the Flies is a novel set in modern times, but suggesting how little progress has as yet been made in the arts of civilisation. Given the chance to make a fresh start, the boys ape their elders and make war on each other because they do not know how to live together in peace.

Golding's second novel, *The Inheritors* (1955), takes us back to a time some fifty or sixty thousand years ago, to the beginnings of civilisation; it is concerned with that period in pre-history when man as we know him today was evolving from his ape-like predecessors. The third novel, *Pincher Martin* (1956), is a twentieth-century tale of survival in which we ostensibly watch the struggles of the title character, Pincher, to survive on a rock in the sea after his ship has been torpedoed.

All of these first three novels are set within very narrow geographical confines: a desert island, a small area of mountain forest and a rock in the middle of the sea, respectively. Golding's fifth novel, *The Spire* (1964), takes place in a similarly restricted setting, the precincts and environs of a great medieval cathedral. Like *The Inheritors* it is set back in time, though, compared to the earlier novel, it is almost modern, belonging historically to the fourteenth century. It is in no way a sociological document, however, and what we learn of the conditions of life at the time is incidental to the main preoccupations of the novel. The spire of the title is the spire of an unnamed medieval cathedral but one which, circumstantially, is very much akin to Salisbury.

Salisbury Cathedral itself was built in about fifty years between 1220 and 1270. Though some authorities (notably the Cathedral guidebook!) put it earlier, the spire was fairly certainly begun about 1334 in the reign of Edward III (1327–77). The action of *The Spire* dates from round about this time and it covers the events of roughly two years during which the building of the spire, begun before the start of the novel, is completed. The primitiveness of life at this period is taken for granted. The filth and the squalor which invade the cathedral, the indifference to human life among the labourers, the sheer anonymity of the 'army' of workmen are all apparent as part of the background, but they are not emphasised or spelled out in any specific way.

The novel has scarcely any story and, on a factual physical level, little plot. The principal interest lies in the moral and spiritual dilemma of the main protagonist, Dean Jocelin. As the building of the spire advances Jocelin climbs upward to watch its progress: simultaneously, we observe his own progression in the spiritual world where he is supposed to be mentor and guide; it is only as he approaches death that he and we realise that the foundations of his life, like those of the cathedral, are based on corruption.

Here, as in all his novels, Golding grapples with the problem of evil; he constantly denies man the easy way out, asserting that evil is not an external force but arises from within us. There will be further discussion of these points in Part 3 of these Notes.

The language of *The Spire* is not easy, for there is no correlation between the comparative simplicity of the vocabulary and the relative obscurity of its underlying meaning. Much of it has a faintly archaic air, fitting its time and setting. The main problems presented by the vocabulary are those of architectural and episcopal terms. The less well-known of these will be explained in Part 2 in the 'Notes and Glossary' following each chapter summary; others may be easily looked up in a good short dictionary such as *The Concise Oxford Dictionary*. Again, there will be further discussion of the language in Part 3 of these Notes.

A note on the text

The textual history of *The Spire* is very straightforward. It is Golding's fifth novel and it was first published by Faber & Faber, London, in 1964; it was republished and put into paperback by the same publishing firm in 1965. In the United States it was first published by Harcourt, Brace & World, New York, in 1964.

Part 2

Summaries
of THE SPIRE

A general summary

In so far as there is a 'story', this novel is about the building of a spire upon a cathedral, the foundations of which are marsh and brushwood. It is about the miraculous resilience of those foundations which, against all the odds, are able to bear the enormous additional weight of a spire some four hundred feet high. It follows the lives and misfortunes of all those who become involved in the building of the spire, from the anonymous army of labourers to the man who believes that he has been chosen by God to put the work in hand. At the end of the novel the spire still stands but its construction has destroyed the lives of Dean Jocelin, whose vision had been the inspiration for its building, of Roger Mason, the master builder, of Roger's wife Rachel, of Pangall the cathedral caretaker, of Pangall's wife Goody and the child she bears to Roger Mason.

We cannot be sure if the spire is the work of God or the work of the devil; we cannot, however, avoid knowing that it is built upon human misery, upon argument and dissension within the cathedral community, and upon the duplicity of Dean Jocelin who holds high office in the church. As the spire reaches upwards Jocelin feels that he bears the weight upon his own back until he is bent double; he suffers, though he does not realise it, from a crippling spinal disease which finally kills him, but throughout the building of the spire he believes that the early physical manifestations of this disease are in fact the visitations of his own guardian angel.

The novel is also concerned with sexuality, with a simple woman unaware of her own attractions, and with two men who desire her; one, Dean Jocelin, suppresses his desires and suffers for it; the other, Roger Mason the master builder, fulfils his desire, gets her with child and also suffers for it. Goody Pangall dies in childbirth; her husband is bullied and ill-treated by Roger's men and finally driven to death as a sacrifice in a cruel pagan rite; Roger tries to kill himself and loses his reason; Rachel is left desolate, tending her helpless husband as though he were the baby they never had; and Jocelin dies in physical and spiritual agony.

Yet at the end the spire still stands – a symbol of what? Of the power of God to work miracles? Of a bargain made with the devil? Or of human skill and endurance? Finally, we cannot tell.

Detailed summaries

Chapter One

The novel begins with Dean Jocelin standing in the cathedral laughing with joy as the sun blazes through a stained-glass window upon him; he holds in his hands a model of the spire which is to be added to the building. The spire represents a fulfilment of his life's hopes. He is in the chapter house with the aged chancellor and they are both looking at a model of the cathedral which has had a square hole cut in it where the spire is to be placed. Their brief conversation informs us that when the spire is completed it will be four hundred feet high. It also introduces us to the doubts which hang over the whole operation, the problem as to whether the foundations of the cathedral are sufficient for the additional weight which will be imposed upon them. Jocelin, however, expresses his faith that God will provide. When the chancellor goes out Jocelin fits the spire on to the model of the cathedral. Here Golding introduces the symbolic comparison between cathedral and man which has continued significance throughout the novel: 'The model was like a man lying on his back. . . . '

Jocelin leaves the chapter house and walks round the cloisters to the west of the cathedral where the building work is proceeding. There, all is noise and confusion, but he observes that, with the alterations taking place, the sun now shines more directly through the windows of the south aisle into the body of the cathedral. A sense of unease is aroused in us by Jocelin's momentary thought that he is standing in a pagan temple, watching priests performing 'some outlandish rite'; he immediately asks forgiveness for this thought but he does not go to pray because he must follow the daily pattern and it is not yet time for prayer. At this moment he sees Pangall's wife, whom he thinks of as his 'daughter in God', enter the cathedral and pass along the north aisle towards the building work; he believes that she is showing her womanly curiosity.

He now becomes aware of another person in his vicinity: Gilbert, the dumb man, is carving a stone head modelled on Jocelin; it is one of four to be placed as gargoyles near the top of the tower upon which the spire will be placed. The dumb man is devoted to the Dean and, throughout the novel, is a little like his shadow, moving around with him, chipping at the stone. Now Jocelin invites the dumb man to follow him to prayer in the Lady Chapel and to continue his work there. As he is about to go to prayer, however, he hears a different noise: the builders have broken through the outer shell of the cathedral, ready for the final stage of their work to begin.

On his way to the Lady Chapel he overhears two young deacons gossiping; we realise, though Jocelin does not, that they are talking about him, accusing him of pride. That he does not connect himself with the subject of their conversation suggests that he is, indeed, too proud to believe anyone can see his actions in a different light from the way he sees them himself. As he goes on he is met by Pangall, the care-taker of the cathedral, a small, rather simple man with a lame left leg. Pangall feels threatened by the building work that is going on; the rough builders bully him, and his little cottage, built against the south wall of the cathedral, is almost inaccessible because of the stone and wood stored in the yard around it. He tells Jocelin that two days pre-viously the workmen killed a man and he fears that they will kill him or drive him away; they jeer at him and strike him so that he is ashamed, even in front of his own wife. As he speaks he begins to shed tears and one drops on Jocelin's shoe; yet Jocelin is embarrassed and able to offer little comfort, except a promise to speak to the master builder. He hurries away from Pangall only to be met by Father Adam the Chap-lain, who wants to deliver a letter to him. This time, however, Jocelin refuses to delay; telling Adam to wait until later, he goes into the Lady Chapel to pray.

Over an hour later, his shins and knees aching from having been kneeling so long, he finishes his prayers. At that moment there is a sen-sation of warmth at his back which he believes to be his 'guardian angel'. Jocelin now stands up, with difficulty, and again becomes aware of his surroundings and of the dumb man sculpting the stone head. He looks at the sculpture and the dumb man attempts to indicate that he is depicting Jocelin as an angel. Pleased, Jocelin turns away and suddenly remembers that Father Adam is waiting with the letter.

A slightly ominous note creeps into the pleasantries the two priests exchange. Jocelin knows that the letter is from his aunt who has contri-buted money for the spire; Father Adam tells him that people believe he can buy favours of the Church through her money. Read aloud by Father Adam, to the accompaniment of the chanting of the Creed from the Lady Chapel, the letter is a plea from Jocelin's aunt that she may be buried in the cathedral; she knows that Jocelin condemns her for having been the King's mistress but hopes that her gift to the cathedral will buy her place there. Jocelin, however, refuses to send an answer to the letter.

This first chapter introduces us to the main protagonist, Dean Joce-lin, and to the principal action, the building of the spire. As the novel progresses we shall observe the close association between the two; Jocelin gradually comes to believe that he bears on his own back the whole burden of the spire. We should notice the heat in his spine after the strain of kneeling; he asserts that he is being warmed by the presence of an angel but later we realise that it is the early signs of a crippling spinal disease. It is not, even at this stage, the only outward sign of corruption within the precincts of the cathedral: Pangall is lame, Gilbert is dumb and the labourers have killed a man.

The constant reference to sun and light which is a feature of this chapter is of considerable significance in the ensuing chapters.

NOTES AND GLOSSARY:

Abraham and Isaac: the story of these two figures, respectively father and son, is told in the Bible, Genesis 22: 1–14. Jocelin sees them carved in stone and illuminated by the sun shining on them through a stained-glass window

chapter house: a building adjoining the cathedral where meetings of the Chapter or governing committee of the cathedral are held

chancellor . . . Lord Chancellor: one of the four Principal Persons or chief religious officers of the cathedral; he is Secretary of the Chapter. (The other three are the Dean, the Sacrist and the Precentor)

Mattins: the service of Morning Prayer

Lady Chapel: the chapel at the east end of the cathedral; dedicated to the Virgin Mary

'Lift up your heads, O ye Gates!': from the Bible, Psalm 24: 7 and 9

High Altar: the principal altar of the cathedral, that is, the altar in the body of the building

chantries: small chapels or altars endowed by donors in order that masses should be sung for their souls

mayfly: any of several winged insects prevalent in the spring

crossways: the central section of the cathedral where the transepts cross the nave; the tower and spire are being built above the crossways

grisaille: here, refers to a row of stained-glass windows

Abel: Abel was the second son of Adam and Eve; he was murdered by his brother Cain (see the Bible, Genesis 4). 'Abel's pillar' was presumably a pillar named after him; there is no such pillar in Salisbury Cathedral

crows: that is, crowbars

interlude: a short medieval play generally enacted between the acts of miracle or morality plays

Peverel chantry: the Hungerford chantry, now in the quire of Salisbury Cathedral, was originally in the nave and was known as the Hungerford-Peverell chantry as it contained the tomb of Catherine Peverell, wife of Walter, Lord Hungerford (mid-fifteenth century)

Glory be: the opening of one of the prayers to the Trinity from *The Book of Common Prayer*, 'Glory be to the Father, and to the Son: and to the Holy Ghost'; also the words which follow the extract from Luke 2 used in the service of Evening Prayer

Hail Mary: the opening words of a set prayer to the Virgin Mary; the reference is to Luke 1:28. Here the words merely imply 'Just a short time ago'

cross-gartered: a medieval fashion of crossing a man's garters above and below the knee in order to keep his stockings in place

wafer thin bricks: the Romans built with thin bricks and in many old Roman towns one can see these bricks, looted from ruined Roman buildings, incorporated into more recent buildings

Therefore with angels and archangels: words from the service of Holy Communion from *The Book of Common Prayer*

Thou has sent ... in the desert: presumably a reference to John the Baptist whose coming was foretold by the prophet Isaiah. See Isaiah 40: 1 and 3, 'Comfort ye, comfort ye my people, saith your God. . . . The voice of him that crieth in the wilderness, Prepare ye the way of the Lord, make straight in the desert a highway for our God.' Mark 1: 2 and 3, 'Behold, I send my messenger before thy face, which shall prepare thy way before thee./The voice of one crying in the wilderness, Prepare ye the way of the Lord, make his paths straight'

With twain he covered ... twain he did fly: from the Bible, Isaiah 6:2. The words are taken from a description of the angelic beings called Seraphim; the translation of the Hebrew word for Seraphim is 'Burners' which clearly has connections with Jocelin's feeling 'the warmth of a fire at his back'

uttering rainwater: the gargoyles or fantastic carved heads projecting from the guttering of medieval churches and cathedrals served the purpose of directing the rainwater from the roof outwards away from the walls; the water poured out from their mouths

sins as scarlet: from the Bible, Isaiah 1: 18 'though your sins be as scarlet, they shall be as white as snow'

I believe in one God: the opening words of the Nicene Creed (statement of articles of belief) used in the service of Holy Communion (see *The Book of Common Prayer*)

cathedral church of the Virgin Mary: the cathedral at Salisbury is the
Cathedral Church of the Blessed Virgin Mary

Of all things visible and invisible: also from the Nicene Creed (see
above)

Suffered under Pontius Pilate: these actual words are from the
Apostles' Creed used at the services of Morning
and Evening Prayer

an earthly king: Jocelin's aunt was the King's mistress; this is presumably a reference to the dissolute King Edward
II (reigned 1307–27). Though some authorities put
it earlier, the building of the spire at Salisbury was
probably completed in 1334 during the reign of
Edward III (1327–77)

render unto Caesar the things which are Caesar's: from the Bible,
Mark 12: 17

To judge the quick and the dead: also from the Apostles' Creed (see
above)

Provoste Chantry: there is no record of a Provoste chantry in Salisbury
Cathedral

The forgiveness of sins and the life everlasting: also from the Apostles'
Creed (see above), though a phrase has been omit-
ted: 'The forgiveness of sins, The Resurrection of
the body, And the life everlasting'

Chapter Two

This chapter also begins with Jocelin bathed in sunlight, though this is
swiftly contrasted with the thick dust surrounding the workmen. He
watches a labourer carrying away some of the rubble and hears him
break into a lewd song; the man ignores Jocelin's reproof, whereat the
Dean rushes into the nave and looks around but there is no cathedral
dignitary on watch; he searches angrily for the Sacrist, Father Anselm,
until, looking across the cloisters, he spies him sitting on a bench in the
sun. Jocelin suppresses his annoyance and points out that no one is on
guard in the nave and that the workmen are singing filthy songs. Father
Anselm replies that the dust is very thick and it affects his chest; he suggests that such songs are minor irritations compared with the enormous
disruption to the daily life of the cathedral brought about by the building work. There is a rise in tension and a latent acrimony is apparent in
the ensuing conversation. Jocelin gets more and more enraged and
finally orders Father Anselm to return to the nave.

Anselm had been one of his oldest friends and now Jocelin begins to
realise that the spire is to cost more than money. He himself goes back
into the cathedral and looks for Roger Mason, the master builder. Roger

is staring down into a pit which has been dug beneath the cathedral and he and a couple of his men are taking measurements; he is clearly disturbed by what he finds. Jocelin, however, tells him that he knew all along that the cathedral lacks foundations and floats on a sort of raft over marshland. Roger tries to insist that the foundations are insufficient to take the weight of the spire; again there is a tension and an undercurrent of anger in the discussion which follows. Jocelin realises that Roger does not wish to continue with the building.

When Pangall comes in Jocelin observes that a workman is limping along behind him, mocking him. Jocelin asks Roger why the men choose to make fun of Pangall but before he can get a satisfactory answer Rachel, Roger's wife, appears, having been attending a service in the Lady Chapel. She starts talking from a distance, bringing the conversation back to the question of the foundations. When she is told that they were talking of Pangall, Rachel makes reference to the fact that both she and Goody Pangall are childless. The men return to the matter of the spire and Jocelin parts from Roger with a final order to him to start to build.

Evening is now coming on and Jocelin begins to make his way out of the cathedral when he is met by Father Adam with another letter. This time it is from the Bishop, who is in Rome, and it contains the promise of a gift, not of money but of a Holy Nail to fix in the spire. Jocelin hurries back to tell Roger Mason this news; the master builder does not appear to be impressed: then, hoping to make peace with Father Anselm, Jocelin goes into the nave to tell him about the Nail. Father Anselm's response is cold and he rebuffs Jocelin's attempt to patch up their quarrel.

That night as he kneels by his bed to pray Jocelin again believes that he feels the warmth of his angel at his back and is comforted.

The tensions which have arisen in this chapter fill us with disquiet. Jocelin's anger and self-centredness make us question the validity of his vision; yet, at the same time, the apparent simplicity of his faith – his belief in the miracle of the cathedral's foundations and the power of the Holy Nail – persuades us that he is a man of God.

NOTES AND GLOSSARY:

Principal Person: see note on chancellor, Chapter One

Chrysostom: St John Chrysostom (345–407). Presumably they are his manuscripts on which the young deacon is working

the new king: presumably King Edward III (reigned 1327–77)

Goody: a familiar form of 'Goodwife'

preaching patriarchs in the clerestory: church fathers and Old Testament figures depicted in the stained-glass windows high over the side aisles

The Holy Father at Rome: the Pope

Chapter Three

Next morning it is raining and it continues to do so for days on end; the river overflows into the city streets and water and slime are everywhere. The workmen stop digging down into the foundations. One day Jocelin sees the master builder lower a lighted candle into the pit which has been dug beneath the cathedral; the pit stinks and the water at the bottom shines in the candle light; it is clear that Roger does not like what he sees. Almost ignoring Jocelin, Roger moodily climbs the corkscrew stair up into the roof. Jocelin is left below and now becomes acutely aware of the smell pervading the whole of the cathedral. As he goes through the crossways, however, he recalls what he believes to be his moment of vision when God told him to build the spire.

The work in the vaulting of the roof continues, accompanied by a sense of stress and anxiety. A workman falls through the hole in the roof and is crushed to death on the stone slabs beneath; the choirboys quarrel with each other; the old chancellor descends into senility; on top of all this there are rumours of plague in the city. This brings more people to mass and Jocelin has the model of the cathedral brought into the crossways to encourage them.

Christmas passes and at last, in March, the weather begins to improve. One day when Jocelin himself needs comfort and encouragement he takes the spire off the model, strokes it and cradles it in his arms. He feels again the excitement and joy of fulfilment and is about to give thanks to God when he sees Goody Pangall come into the cathedral. She is looking, with obvious terror, sideways over the crossways and Jocelin, looking in the same direction, sees Roger Mason coming towards her.

Roger crosses to Goody and Jocelin watches as she repeatedly shakes her head but is, nevertheless, unable to break away from him and go on her way to the market. Jocelin realises with horror that something is going on between the master builder and Goody Pangall; he is overwhelmed with grief and indignation and, the model spire still in his hands, he rushes out of the cathedral gasping for breath. The workmen jeer at him so that he returns to the crossways only to meet Rachel Mason carrying a baby into the christening service. Though he must know that the baby is not hers he mechanically congratulates and blesses her; the baby is snatched away by another woman and Rachel remains behind to shock him with an absurd explanation of her sex life and why she cannot have a child. When she leaves him Jocelin finds himself almost unable to subdue his own sexual reactions and cries out 'Filth! Filth!' at the very moment when Pangall appears, and is overheard by the caretaker.

Pangall is still distressed at the way he is treated by the workmen;

Jocelin tries to tell him that he will have sons who will rejoice in the building of the spire done in their father's day but Pangall himself knows that he is impotent and limps angrily away.

Still shaken by his knowledge of the relationship between Goody Pangall and Roger Mason, Jocelin kneels to pray but only thoughts of sex come into his mind; we realise, though at this stage he does not, that he is dominated by sexual jealousy, that he, in fact, desires his 'daughter in God' but has suppressed his desires. He tries to pray for strength for Goody Pangall but is overcome by an evil thought which presses upon him: Goody will help to keep the master builder working on the cathedral. Jocelin returns to the deanery, dazed by his willingness to admit sin if it serves his own ends. When he goes to bed he feels the warmth at his back and falls asleep but is tormented by terrible nightmares in which Goody Pangall appears as Satan and works at the building. He awakes and mortifies his flesh by lashing himself; he then sleeps again, this time, his penance done, more peacefully.

The spiritual conflict, symbolised by Satan and the angel, now begins to appear more overtly and we are forced to ask ourselves many questions: is the spire being built to the glory of God or to the glory of Jocelin? Is it possible for God to be glorified by an end achieved through evil means? Can Good come out of Evil? Is Jocelin being tested as was Abraham (to whom reference was made in Chapter One)? Does God demand the burden of sin as a proof of obedience? Or is Jocelin fallible, sinful man masquerading as a saint? Furthermore, a sexual theme has entered the novel; now the spire corresponds to the phallus so that the building of it becomes for Jocelin some sort of sexual achievement, a spiritual masturbation: notice how he strokes the model of the spire.

NOTES AND GLOSSARY:

'... I received what I received ... on my face': the explanation of Jocelin's words here is to be found in Chapter Ten

'Lord, let our cry come unto thee!: from *The Book of Common Prayer*, the Confirmation Service: 'Lord, hear our prayers. And let our cry come unto thee'

the Host: the bread consecrated as the body of Christ and used in the service of Mass or Holy Communion

Let the heavens rejoice ... because he cometh: see the Bible, I Chronicles 16: 31–3: 'Let the heavens be glad, and let the earth rejoice... Then shall the trees of the wood sing out at the presence of the Lord, because he cometh...'

Zany: a buffoon who was not the Fool himself but an attendant on the Fool, imitating, often incompetently, the Fool's clowning

pig's bladder:	a pig's bladder inflated and fixed to a stick was the 'balloon' of the old medieval Fools and clowns; it was often used to create vulgar mirth
a discipline:	an ecclesiastical term for a punishment ordained to punish a wrongdoer

Chapter Four

Jocelin now busies himself about his ecclesiastical work, visiting the churches in the city and those in the countryside around. The people are depressed for it is a time of famine and disease and the winter has been hard. At last, however, the rains abate, the floodwaters recede and a fresh wind clears the air. The old chancellor dies and a new young one is installed. New hope appears with the coming of spring, yet Jocelin is helpless to combat the lewd songs, the mocking of Pangall or the affair between Goody and Roger. Then one day in Lent he enters the cathedral to find that a hole has been made in the roof where the spire is to be built. As the work progresses there are complaints that the noise disturbs the services in the Lady Chapel, so Jocelin himself climbs up to see what is being done. A hundred and twenty feet up in the vaulting he looks down with fascination and excitement at the world beneath him; then he sees that the new building has begun and he is overjoyed. After Easter, with the better weather, the tower rises swiftly. The forester who has been providing the huge beams is rewarded by being made a minor canon or church dignitary in a special installation ceremony and the work continues.

With the dry weather the dust returns but Pangall has lost heart and no longer bothers to clear up. By now Gilbert, the dumb man, has completed three of the four heads of the Dean. Jocelin is obsessed with watching the progress of the work. One day he sees Roger Mason arguing with some of his men at the top of the building. After this, Roger comes down and prepares an experiment to see if the four pillars of the crossways are sinking; it appears, however, that they are not. Jocelin observes all that is going on and has the uneasy presentiment that trouble will follow.

One day early in June when Jocelin arrives in the cathedral there are no workmen there. He looks around and finds them outside the north transept in the huge shed that had housed the beams throughout the winter; he thinks that they are asking for an increase in their wages. The crisis is more serious than this, however: they do not want to continue with the work. Shortly afterwards, whilst Jocelin is in the Lady Chapel trying to pray, the dumb man comes to fetch him to the crossways. Everyone is assembled there and Roger Mason and his assistant Jehan are crouched down looking into the pit which is illuminated by an ingenious system of trapping the sun's beams on a sheet of metal and reflecting them obliquely downwards.

As Jocelin kneels beside Roger he is horrified to see that the whole of the bottom of the pit is moving as if there were millions of grubs crawling about in it. To the men looking down it seems to be the mouth of hell. Then bits of stone from the cathedral itself begin to break off and fall into the pit. Simultaneously the whole structure of the building appears to ring or sing on a high-pitched note. The master builder quickly takes control and orders everyone to collect stones and fill the pit with them; the workmen rush to do his bidding and among the stones thrown down are the dumb man's heads of Dean Jocelin.

Whilst they are trying to fill in the pit Jocelin goes into the choir and kneels as near to the centre of the arch above the crossways as he can get. He does not pray in the normal sense but feels his spirit struggling in conflict with Satan. He remains thus, unconscious of what is happening around him, until he comes to believe that the whole building rests on his back. When he returns to full consciousness again the ringing of the stones has ceased and Roger Mason is standing before him. Roger declares that the building work must now stop since it is clear that the cathedral has no foundations and could not support a spire. Jocelin accuses him of having waited until building work is available at Malmesbury. An argument between them ensues in which both men are acutely conscious that it is not only the building of the spire which is at stake but also the reputation of Goody Pangall; it is Jocelin who decides that she must be sacrificed to his vision. Jocelin's dominance is apparent through the language of this passage which symbolises Roger as an animal and Jocelin as controlling a trap. Having shut the escape route by writing to the Abbot of Malmesbury telling him that Roger and his men are not available, Jocelin shuts the trap with a final 'Click' and forces the master builder to go on with the work.

Roger leaves him and Jocelin, feeling exhausted, realises that he must go to his bed. He gets up from his knees and makes his way through the crossways where he sees the workmen mocking Pangall as usual; one of them fixes the model spire between his legs like a monstrous phallus. Pangall breaks down and rushes away howling, whereat the whole pack chase him, pushing their way past Jocelin whom the dumb man protects with his own body. As the Dean crouches, shuddering, the sight of Goody Pangall impresses itself on his mind; her hair is dishevelled, her dress torn down the front and she is looking in anguish across to Roger Mason.

We do not realise until later that Pangall has been driven into the pit and is dead; he is a symbolic sacrifice to the work in hand. Jocelin, however, has sacrificed Goody too; yet he continues to believe that he is fulfilling God's will in insisting that the spire is built. In the chapters which follow we shall find ourselves questioning who really won in Jocelin's struggle with Satan. Was it Jocelin who won and himself supports the building through his faith? Or did Satan win Jocelin's soul in exchange for the miracle of holding up the spire? Like Jesus he had been 'on a pinnacle of the temple' (see the Bible, Luke 4: 9), but whilst Jesus put temptation to sin behind him, Jocelin appears to have succumbed to it.

The progression of the disease in Jocelin's spine is very noticeable in this chapter for it is alluded to not only through the warmth of the presence of the angel but also through the pain and sickness that Jocelin experiences when he kneels to look into the pit.

NOTES AND GLOSSARY:

in his gift: an ecclesiastical term, here meaning that Jocelin was able to appoint the clergy to these churches

Church of Saint Thomas: the original Church of St Thomas in Salisbury was built before the end of the thirteenth century; little of the original church remains

'I am about my Father's business': see the Bible, Luke 2: 49, the words of Jesus, 'wist ye not that I must be about my Father's business?'

Lent: the period of six and a half weeks between Ash Wednesday and Easter Sunday; the forty weekdays in this period are ordained as days of fasting and self-denial

checkers: draughts; a game played with a chequered board and black and white counters

'Rejoice, O daughters of Jerusalem': see the Bible, Zechariah 9: 9, 'Rejoice greatly, O daughter of Zion; shout, O daughter of Jerusalem'; this comes from the passage foretelling the kingship of Christ reported in the Bible, Luke 19: 28–40

the grave waited. . . . He is arisen: see the Bible, Matthew 28: 5–6; 'And the angel answered and said unto the women, Fear not ye: for I know that ye seek Jesus, which was crucified. He is not here: for he is risen'

St Aldhelm: Aldhelm (639–709) became Abbot of Malmesbury in 675. His life is not now depicted in any of the stained-glass windows at Salisbury but there is a post-war statue of him in the South Quire aisle

tythe barn: more commonly 'tithe'. The old tithe-tax levied a tenth of a man's produce or labour to support the church; a tithe barn was a barn built to hold the tithes paid in kind

clock figures ... hour to strike:	a reference to the kind of old clocks in churches and town centres where a procession of figures comes out on the hour to perform
a defensive sign:	the sign of the cross to ward off evil
Dia Mater:	(*Latin*) Mother of God
key of the arch:	an architectural term indicating the centre of the arch which takes the stress of the weight of the archway from all directions
Malmesbury:	a town in Wiltshire; part of the twelfth-century Abbey-Church still survives after many centuries of alteration and restoration
a refiner's fire:	see the Bible, Malachi 3: 2, 'for he is like a refiner's fire'; this is a reference to the Day of Judgement when Christ shall sit in judgement over men

Chapter Five

Somehow Jocelin reaches his own room but there follow weeks of delirium when the events of that terrible day are confused in his mind. Then he awakes one morning and is better. It is now September and, despite Father Adam's protestations, he goes to see how the work is progressing. He is not fully recovered in body or mind; he walks unsteadily, is short of breath and nervous tension causes him to giggle when he speaks. He sees Roger Mason who ignores him and climbs up into the tower.

Jocelin looks around the crossways and sees a lot of dust, dirt and mess; for a moment he wonders where Pangall is and then he remembers Father Adam telling him that the caretaker has disappeared. He thinks of Goody, left alone, and decides he must give her some help. At this point, as he stands beside one of the pillars, he looks down; he sees a twig with a rotting berry on it lying across his shoes; he shakes it off in disgust but it is only much later (see Chapter Eight) that he realises its significance; now, he merely worries that the wood being used for the building may be unseasoned so that the spire will warp and perhaps sprout. As he looks up he sees that the building is getting on well; even a little hut has appeared, like a swallow's nest, near the top of the work. Then he observes the dumb man, with a new piece of stone, working at his head again. Jocelin embraces the young man and thanks him for saving his life. When he addresses him as 'My son' he remembers Goody Pangall, his 'daughter in God' and groans aloud.

Day by day Jocelin grows stronger and as he recovers he feels that it is his will that supports the growing spire. Goody Pangall appears to avoid him but Roger's wife Rachel always comes to talk to him; he at last comes to the conclusion that the best way to deal with her is to ignore her completely; then he discovers that this is an excellent way to treat everyone.

When the dumb man has completed two heads Jocelin sees them and thinks they are too thin and not very like him. By December all four heads are finished and taken up the tower. Jocelin again thinks that he must help Goody and one day, arms outspread, he detains her but she begs him to let her go. He tries to tell her that her husband will return and then he says that she is very dear to him; this remark distresses her immeasurably and, escaping from him, she hurries away. He cannot understand what has happened and tries to lose himself in thoughts of the spire. He begins to climb up the ladders to the tower; some way up he meets Roger Mason who is in angry mood but again Jocelin cannot understand why. He goes on climbing until he reaches the very top of the building work; there he sees the dumb man, preparing to place the four heads in position.

High up in the tower Jocelin feels free; he hears the wind blowing through the building and suddenly he feels the burden of the spire on his own back again. This makes him recollect once more Pangall being mocked by the workmen and Goody with her hair loose and her dress torn; he is aware again how much the spire is costing but he cannot pray.

From where he is standing Jocelin looks down at the world beneath him and wishes the spire could be a thousand feet high so that he could see over the whole county. Now he is full of joy and kneels to pray but his mind is suddenly occupied with the ills and evils of life and his prayer is only for forgiveness. He opens his eyes and continues to watch what is happening below when Roger, who has climbed up behind him, becomes angry because he can see a barge carrying stone for the work and the bargeman has gone into an alehouse. Jocelin follows Roger down the ladders and is met at the bottom by Rachel chattering as usual; she mentions, almost incidentally, that Goody is pregnant. When he hears this Jocelin is overcome with anger and distress; he feels that God has deceived him, because he had believed Pangall to be impotent. In a sneering prayer, using words from the Bible, he thanks God for giving the barren Goody a child.

The burden of the spire is, indeed, on Jocelin's back, though not miraculously. He himself, however, still does not realise that by forcing Roger Mason to stay at the cathedral he has sacrificed Goody Pangall. The end of the chapter seems to suggest that he has some doubts as to whether the building of the spire is entirely God's will, and whether it has been done at too great a cost. Notice the twig with its rotting berry that lies across Jocelin's shoe; not only is it another sign of the corruption within the cathedral but also it acquires much greater significance for Jocelin later on.

NOTES AND GLOSSARY:

'My son, my son!': see the Bible, II Samuel 18: 33. King David's son Absalom has been killed and when David hears of his death he cries out, 'O my son Absalom, my son, my son Absalom! Would God I had died for thee, O Absalom, my son, my son!'

graver: engraving or sculpting tool

Stilbury: this appears to be an invented name as there is no Stilbury close to Salisbury. It could be a reference to either Amesbury or Wilton, though neither of these places quite fits in with the facts given us about Stilbury. Wilton, which is about three miles from Salisbury, is the most likely origin though it is to the north west, not the north east of Salisbury; there was a famous Benedictine nunnery there in the Middle Ages

though they were enclosed: the nuns belonged to what is known as an 'Enclosed Order' which means that they are not allowed to go outside their convent

remembering Saint John: 'It is an eagle': see the Bible, the Revelation of Saint John the Divine. There are two references to flying eagles in Revelation; the first is at 4: 7 but the second at 12: 14 is more relevant, for there a woman is given the wings of an eagle to escape from Satan

'Thou hast remembered Thy handmaiden': see the Bible, I Samuel 1. Hannah, the wife of Elkanah, is childless. She makes a vow to God that, if he will grant her, his 'handmaid', a son, she will give that son back to God's service. In verse 19 it is recorded that 'the Lord remembered her'; she gave birth to a son who became the prophet Samuel

Chapter Six

Work on the spire progresses slowly during the dark days of winter; sometimes on foggy days the labourers are unable to climb up to work on the spire itself but spend their time preparing wood below. Jocelin observes that Roger has become unpopular with the men because of his uneven temper; yet the master builder carries stolidly on with his work, using his instruments and often standing to listen. The stones of the cathedral have begun to sing again intermittently; people from far and wide come to listen to them, always standing by the great west door without going into the cathedral. The workmen have lost their cheerfulness and one day Jocelin realises that Roger Mason is afraid as he climbs the tower. When Jocelin taxes him with his fear Roger begs to be allowed to stop the work; the Dean, however, insists that it is God's work and must go on. He tells Roger that it is not he, the Dean, speaking, but God speaking through him. The master builder now has the idea of fixing a steel band round the whole tower to hold it secure; he explains that it will cost a lot more money and Jocelin promises to find it.

About a month later the committee of Chapter meets and refuses to approve the extra money, so the Dean has to seal the documents with his own private seal. After the meeting, feeling weary and depressed, Jocelin decides to climb up the tower where he always feels happy. As he climbs he hears a moan and, approaching the hut that has been built halfway up, he sees Roger Mason's hand gripping a beam of wood; then it is covered by another – that of Goody Pangall – and he hears her say, 'But I didn't laugh – did I?' Jocelin remembers Rachel Mason telling him that she would never have a child because she always laughed at the crucial moment of intercourse; he realises with a shock of horror that Roger and Goody have been copulating in the hut. Jocelin is distraught for he now understands that Roger is the father of the child about to be born. Memories of Goody as an innocent child flood in on him. The true cost of the spire is more than he had bargained for. He hastens down the ladders to be met by Rachel who has been looking for Roger. Jocelin blesses her mechanically and goes to his deanery to pray. By the next day the hut has been removed.

As the novel proceeds it becomes increasingly obvious that it is less about the building of the spire than about the passions and emotions behind it and particularly about the burning ambition of Dean Jocelin to see it finished. In this chapter we are presented with two possibilities: Jocelin's belief that God is speaking and working through him and Roger's suspicion that Jocelin is the 'devil himself'.

NOTES AND GLOSSARY:

muted whitely: the use of the archaic word 'mute' instead of the vulgar word 'shit' or the more sophisticated 'defecate' is not only more suited to the precincts of the cathedral but is also a punning contrast to the 'shouting' of the faces themselves

capstone: architectual term for the top stone which crowns a building

to build a ship on dry land: see the Bible, Genesis 6–8, the story of the flood and Noah's ark

to sit among the dunghills: perhaps a reference to the Bible, Jonah 3: 6, 'For word came unto the king of Nineveh, and he arose from his throne . . . and covered him with sackcloth and sat in ashes.' The Hebrew word translated as 'dunghills' also means 'ashes' or 'ash-heaps'

to marry a whore: see the Bible, Hosea 1: 2 'the Lord said unto Hosea, Go, take unto thee a wife of whoredoms'

to set their son on the altar of sacrifice: see the Bible, Genesis 22, the story of Abraham offering his son Isaac to God as a sacrifice

Chapter Seven

Jocelin's thoughts are disturbed by thoughts of Goody Pangall and he knows that they are prurient thoughts. He tries to escape them by climbing the ladders up to the tower but escape is impossible. When he goes down again he hears the master builder in the north transept explaining to his men the part each has to play in helping to affix the steel band around the tower. Jocelin cannot, however, get Goody out of his mind; he returns to his room and writes to the Abbess of Stilbury asking her to take in 'a poor, fallen woman'. Then he returns to watch the progress of the work. Smoke and sparks arise from the top of the tower where the steel band is being bent and riveted to the stone. When this work is finished and the workmen go wearily away to sleep, Jocelin climbs the tower again; he falls asleep at the top; on awakening he slowly becomes aware that the tower is swaying in the wind. He is terrified but keeps himself under control; he goes down to the crossways and, dedicating the work to God, returns to his deanery.

He now learns that the Abbess of Stilbury will receive Goody Pangall but only with a sizeable dowry; he realises that she believes the child to be his. He takes some money, however, and makes his way to Pangall's cottage. Hs is about to enter when Rachel Mason darts past him into the cottage, and screaming and shouting arise from inside. Then the door opens and Roger stumbles out, blood streaming from his head, with Rachel, a broom in her hand, in hot pursuit. Jocelin goes to the door of the cottage with the money and looks in. Goody is kneeling before the fire; when she sees him she screams and holds her belly; then she screams again and again. He drops the money and rushes for help, realising that she is in labour. Some of the workmen go to help and Jocelin returns to see the money on the floor stained with blood. He has to baptise the newborn and probably already dead baby and Father Anselm comes to administer the last rites to Goody Pangall. Jocelin staggers away to kneel in the choir and pray but his prayer is a strange one for the Dean of a cathedral: he tries to make a bargain with God for Goody's life; now, at last, too, he faces the decision he made a year earlier when he first learned that there was something between Roger and Goody. He again becomes delirious and many hours later

Father Adam finds him crouching in the same place and tells him that Goody Pangall is dead.

This comparatively short chapter is a turning-point both in the building work and in Jocelin himself. First, the steel band is fitted round the tower successfully and, though it sways in the wind, the building still stands. Secondly, Jocelin is forced to accept responsibility for what has happened between Goody and Roger and to realise that the cost of the spire is more than he had bargained for; the cost in human suffering and misery now impinges itself clearly upon his mind.

NOTES AND GLOSSARY:

there was blood over the money on the floor: through this reference Jocelin is being compared with Judas who betrayed Christ for thirty pieces of silver, 'the price of blood'; see the Bible, Matthew 27: 3–10

a reed shaken in the wind: see the Bible, Luke 7: 24. This is a significant reference because it is Christ's description of what John the Baptist was not; he goes on to say that John was a prophet 'and much more than a prophet'. The reference suggests that Jocelin is not a prophet, that his vision is faulty

beldame: an archaic word used here to suggest the witchcraft of sex and of women's allurement

This have I done for my true love: these words come from the carol 'My Dancing Day'; the words and music are by Sandys and date from 1833. See *The Oxford Book of Carols*. This carol is occasionally sung at Salisbury Cathedral

---

Chapter Eight

Goody Pangall is buried and Jocelin has a mental and emotional breakdown. He wanders about aimlessly, repeating words and phrases over and over again. Physically, too, his condition deteriorates, his whole body gradually being taken over by the disease that is within him.

Roger and Rachel are back together again and she acts more than ever like his keeper, whilst he appears to have lost his purpose in living. Jocelin himself is obsessed with the memory of Goody but it is always her white body, the blood and 'the terrible christening' that come into his mind. When he tries to remember her as a child his thoughts constantly revert to his last sight of her.

Now he neglects his church work and devotes himself to the building of the spire, climbing up among the workmen to try to forget what has happened. He discovers that Roger has taken to drink and now much of the work is organised by his assistant, Jehan. The spire continues to rise; Jocelin spends more and more of his time with the workmen who are glad to see him up the tower with them because they feel he brings them good luck.

A day comes when Jehan borrows Roger's plumb-line and goes down to ground level; he returns to report that the columns in the crossways are bending. Suddenly Roger breaks down; moaning oddly and ignoring everyone, he climbs down the ladders and goes away; all the workmen laugh and jeer and Jocelin promises them more money if they get on with the job. He himself observes that the pillars are indeed bending but he notices that the more they bend the less they sing. By midsummer, however, both bending and singing seem to have ceased. The work speeds up; Jocelin takes an active part, helping in such tasks as directing the metal sheet used as a mirror. He begins to confide in the men, telling them first about his angel, which seems not to surprise them, and then about his vision, which they do not understand. He talks of the sermon he intends to preach when the spire is finished and the dumb man offers to carve the pulpit.

Then one day the men finish work early and, refusing to respond to Jocelin's pleas, they go away. After wandering about aimlessly for a while, he again climbs the ladders and, as the evening lengthens and darkness approaches, he sees fires all round on the horizon. Suddenly he understands why the men have gone: it is Midsummer Eve and they have gone to join in the devil worship around the blazing midsummer fires. He is greatly distressed; his mind roams back to memories he would rather forget and particularly at this moment to the twig with the rotting berry on it that had lain across his shoe. He now believes this to have been mistletoe and thinks he must be bewitched. He goes down to the crossways and feels the paving stones there burning his feet like the fires of hell.

It is by now clear to the reader that Dean Jocelin, for all his angels and visions, is no saint. Yet, until the death of Goody Pangall he was convinced that he was fulfilling God's will. He is no longer sure, and the knowledge that the men who are building God's spire are also anxious to placate the devil causes him anguish. At the same time, magic becomes another scapegoat for him as he declares himself to be 'bewitched'.

NOTES AND GLOSSARY:

widdershins: (*dialect*) in an anti-clockwise direction; this is associated with bad luck or evil; witches move widdershins round their cauldrons!

Visitor: an official appointed by ecclesiastical authorities to inspect and check on the activities at the cathedral in order to prevent any irregularities

as Mahomet's tomb, off centre: Mahomet (*c*.570–632) was buried in Medina. The 'centre' of Islam, to which all Moslems turn when they pray, is Kaaba in Mecca. Thus, Mahomet's tomb may be considered to be 'off centre'

Midsummer Night: Midsummer was one of the principal festivals of the Druids who were popularly believed to worship the devil. It was celebrated with bonfires and originally with human sacrifice. Many of the traditions were carried on long after the religion itself had died out

the valley of the Hanging Stones: probably a reference to Clearbury Ring; Stonehenge is too far away from Salisbury

David . . . blood on his hands: see the Bible, I Chronicles 22: 7–8, 'And David said to Solomon, My son, as for me, it was in my mind to build an house unto the name of the Lord my God: But the word of the Lord came to me saying . . . thou shalt not build an house unto my name, because thou hast shed much blood upon the earth in my sight.' The particular act of David that must have been in Jocelin's mind was his deliberate sending of Uriah the Hittite to death in order that he could marry Uriah's wife, Bathsheba (see II Samuel 11)

Mistletoe: used by the Druids in their Midsummer festival. The Druids, dressed in white robes, cut it with a golden sickle and collected it in a white cloth. Mistletoe was believed to have magic powers, one of which was to help fertility. It is a parasitic plant and causes abnormal growths known as 'witches' brooms' on the branches of the host tree

---

Chapter Nine

After the Midsummer festivities Jocelin is more inhibited with the workmen but he continues to encourage them and they draw comfort from his presence. The year wears on and late summer gales come, with raging winds and rain. At last Jocelin, from high up in the spire, sees the Visitor with a long procession approaching from fifteen miles away with the Holy Nail. Its arrival is timely for Jehan is about to set the spire in place. The capstone is fitted to the top of the cone; then, by an ingenious method originally devised by Roger Mason, the spire – all one hundred and fifty feet of it – is dropped into position. The noise, the vibrations, the shock of the operation is terrifying and everyone believes that the whole edifice is about to fall. At that moment the Nail arrives and Jocelin takes it to the High Altar for dedication. He is anxious to place it in the spire but is compelled to see the Visitor and his committee first.

The ensuing interview is a little like a trial, for the Visitor has received a number of complaints which have been lodged against Jocelin. He appears less and less able to answer the questions put to him but it does transpire that he has not been to Confession for two years or more. The Visitor then orders him to return to his room which he does, accompanied by Father Adam. The weather is still wild and once in his room Jocelin begs Adam to go and tell them that the Nail must be driven in, in order to make the spire safe. Adam does not return and after a while Jocelin drops into a deep sleep.

He is awakened by cries and screams; emerging from his room he finds that the storm is raging worse than ever; the people believe that the city is being destroyed and beg him to pray for them. He determines to fix the Nail in place and thus to thwart Satan's attacks on the spire. In his weak state he is blown and buffeted by the wind and beaten to his knees as he makes his way to the High Altar; he takes the silver box containing the Holy Nail and stumbles, crawls and scrabbles up the ladders to the top of the spire where he beats the Nail into the wood. He believes now that the spire is safe; he goes down the ladders again and falls on his face in the ambulatory with the winds howling round him like devils. He then has a vision or daydream in which he sees a sunlit view across the close where three devils disguised as little girls are dancing and singing the old rhyme, 'For want of a nail the shoe was lost'. He, a young man, walks across to them and calls a little red-haired girl to him. Naked, she approaches him; though he cannot see her face it is, of course, Goody Pangall but she smiles and hums like the dumb man. They come together in a mystic consummation which releases his tensions and he lapses into unconsciousness.

Has the spire been completed by God's will, or by the devil's co-operation, or merely by the supreme skill of a master builder and his army of workmen? We do not know but, contrary to all expectation, it stands. Jocelin clearly believes that Satan is angry and frustrated and has sent his devils to destroy the cathedral. Once the Nail is in place he feels the spire is safe and, as he relaxes, he is assailed by his own weak, fallible, human nature; in a moment of vision or imagination he achieves sexual fulfilment as he lies exhausted.

NOTES AND GLOSSARY:

feathers: quill pens

' — now and in the hour of — ': from a prayer to the Virgin Mary: 'Holy Mary, Mother of God, pray for us now and in the hour of our death.'

For want of a nail... the kingdom was lost: the earliest reference to this rhyme given in *The Oxford Dictionary of Nursery Rhymes* dates from 1629 in one of Thomas Adams's *Sermons*: 'The want of a nail loseth the shoe, the loss of a shoe troubles the horse, the horse endangereth the rider, the rider breaking his ranks molests the company so far as to hazard the whole army.'

Chapter Ten

When Jocelin comes to himself again it is already the next morning. The events of the preceding night have given him a new understanding, though he has not come to terms with it. He gets up and walks to the crossways where he is met by Father Adam who tells him that his aunt Alison is waiting to speak to him. Remembering that she had been the King's mistress, Jocelin thinks she may be able to tell him something of the sexual urge within him and agrees to see her.

He goes with Adam to the deanery where Alison is sitting in a chair by the log fire. Her women withdraw from the room but Father Adam remains. She tells her nephew that she has come because she has heard of his troubles; yet, despite his new knowledge, he still despises her way of life and suggests that her help may defile him; this momentarily angers her. Jocelin, however, tries to explain to her that he was chosen by God to build the spire. Alison is overcome with laughter and tells him the true story of his rise in the church – that after intercourse with the king he offered her a present and she asked for preferment for her nephew. Jocelin is devastated but holds on to the fact that the Bishop sent him a Nail to help secure the spire. Alison swiftly puts this into perspective: 'You asked him for money – and he sent you a nail!' At this Jocelin is overcome by his sickness; then he feels her taking his hands and urging him to have faith and to believe in his vocation. Now he remembers what he had wanted to ask her; he tells her of his obsession with Goody Pangall and begs her to explain whether it is witchcraft. Alison is now shocked in her turn and retreats from him whispering that it is indeed witchcraft.

When she has gone and he is left with Father Adam he moans and mutters to himself. Some hours later the dumb man comes to them and persuades them to look at the pillars at the crossways; he has discovered that, though they seem to bear the weight of the spire, they are merely shells packed with rubble! The horror that his vision and his 'angel' are evil comes upon him and at that moment his diseased back gives way and he collapses on the stone floor; symbolically, his angel throws off his disguise, pushes aside the two wings that are hiding his cloven hoof and strikes him with a white hot flail. Jocelin is carried back to his own bed where he lies in delirium, periodically asking Father Adam if the spire still stands.

In an effort to make clear his reasons for building the spire, Jocelin now asks Adam to read the notebook in which he had recorded his vision. Adam reads, to an accompaniment of comments from Jocelin. When Adam has finished reading, it is clear that he is not convinced by the vision. He fears that Jocelin has never been taught to pray and after praying himself he tries to teach the Dean the stages of prayer; Jocelin can only cry out, however, that his spire pierced every stage and he is again wracked with pain.

Jocelin's physical disease has now reached its climax; it is paralleled by his spiritual sickness. He hopes that his aunt Alison, once the King's mistress, will be able to help him to understand his sexual obsession, but, whilst she can accept her own laxity, she cannot accept it in Jocelin, her 'father in God'. Father Adam, too, though he is only the Dean's chaplain, rejects Jocelin's vision and feels that his life as Dean has been a sham. Thus, he is rejected by representatives of both the secular and the spiritual world. It at last appears that Jocelin has been misled by his vision and that his 'angel' is a devil in disguise.

NOTES AND GLOSSARY:

ogival: architectural term for a moulded S-shaped curve

cast myself headlong on these stones: is this a reference to the temptations of Christ? St Matthew tells us that in the second of these temptations the devil took Jesus and set him on the pinnacle of the temple and bade him, 'cast thyself down: for it is written, He shall give his angels charge concerning thee; and in their hands they shall bear thee up, lest at any time thou dash thy foot against a stone' (Matthew 11: 6)

'It were better a millstone were tied about their necks': see the Bible, Matthew 18: 6, 'But whoso shall offend one of these little ones which believe in me, it were better for him that a millstone were hanged about his neck, and that he were drowned in the depth of the sea.'

giants . . . in those days: see the Bible, Genesis 6: 4

cloven hoof: the devil can be recognised by his cloven hooves

Hair blown back . . . but for hosannahs: a reference to the dumb man's heads of Jocelin; see Chapter One

Chapter Eleven

Jocelin's lucid intervals become fewer and fewer but, whenever he is able to think, he asks if the spire has yet fallen. One day he sends for

Anselm, but Jocelin is no longer Dean so Anselm does not bother to come until Jocelin sends a second message begging him to come for charity's sake. Though Jocelin tries to explain himself and asks forgiveness, Anselm is stiff and unfriendly; moreover, he is bitterly critical of Jocelin whose swift climb through the ecclesiastical hierarchy he has long envied. Though he knows that Jocelin is a sick and dying man, Anselm is spiteful and resentful; he goes away, having paid only lip-service to Jocelin's request for forgiveness.

Jocelin is now desperately anxious to seek forgiveness of those he feels he has offended; his interviews with Alison and with Anselm have been unsuccessful but he decides to search out Roger Mason. He knows that he will have to leave his house when Father Adam is not watching and he does so with considerable cunning. He can hardly move but, having tricked Adam into thinking he is asleep, he crawls downstairs, finds a stick and manages to stumble outside. There he smells a sweet scent and looks up where he believes at first that he sees a cloud of angels with a serpent among them; it is an appletree with a 'witches' broom' of mistletoe among its branches. Then he sees a kingfisher by the river and calls for it to come back but it does not return.

Jocelin now goes out into the High Street and, by dint of asking many times, finds his way to the place where Roger Mason lodges. He is so exhausted by his efforts that he can do no more until Rachel helps him up to Roger's room. The master builder has changed; he is completely dissipated and a physical wreck. Jocelin tries to explain himself to Roger and asks his forgiveness; for a while there is harmony between them until Jocelin talks of the death of Pangall and of Goody. When he goes on to suggest that in some way he was responsible for Goody's death, Roger gets angrier and angrier until he throws Jocelin out of his room and down the stairs. There Jocelin is set on by an angry mob and buffeted and beaten. Later, Rachel and Father Adam come and carry him gently back to the deanery.

As the novel draws towards its end we realise that, although the spire still stands, Jocelin's 'vision' has been almost totally destructive. First and foremost, it has destroyed Jocelin himself; it has disrupted the services within the cathedral; it has brought about the deaths (among others) of Pangall and his wife; it has helped to corrupt Anselm and it has caused the downfall of Roger Mason. The 'glory' of the cathedral has been built out of human ruin.

The appletree and mistletoe, representatives respectively of biblical doctrine and pagan superstition, are inextricably bound together in this chapter, just as they seem to have had a confused influence upon the building and builders of the spire. Jocelin would clearly like to shelve responsibility for the evil he has found within himself, to blame original sin and Man's fall from grace, or, alternatively to blame witchcraft, but he knows that such explanations are 'too simple' and that 'they're all mixed up'.

NOTES AND GLOSSARY:

'In the midst of life — ': from *The Book of Common Prayer*, the service for the Burial of the Dead, 'In the midst of life we are in death.'

'You tempted me and I did eat': see the Bible, Genesis 3: 12, Adam's excuse to God for disobeying him and eating of the tree of the Knowledge of Good and Evil, 'The woman whom thou gavest to be with me, she gave me of the tree, and I did eat.'

kingfisher: the episode of the kingfisher may be a reference to Bernard Shaw's *St Joan* (1923). Dunois and his page see a kingfisher and Dunois connects the bird with the Virgin Mary, 'Mary in the blue snood, kingfisher colour'. It is the precursor of Joan's arrival and of an apparently miraculous wind-change which enables the French to recapture Orleans. Like Jocelin, Joan believed that she was guided by angels

mounting block: a block of stone at the side of a roadway for horse-men to stand on, more easily to mount their horses

morse: the clasp of a cape

An eye for an eye, tooth for tooth: see the Bible, Exodus 21: 24, 'Eye for eye, tooth for tooth'; this is part of the explica-tion of God's law in the Old Testament. Jesus in the New Testament rejected this harsh justice: see Matthew 5: 38—9, 'Ye have heard that it hath been said, An eye for an eye, and a tooth for a tooth: But I say unto you, That ye resist not evil: but who-soever shall smite thee on thy right cheek, turn to him the other also.'

Chapter Twelve

Broken physically and spiritually, Jocelin is taken back to his bed. He is desperately troubled and no longer capable of connected thought. To help to relieve his pain and induce sleep he is given a bitter drink which he guesses is poppy juice or opium. A succession of days and nights pass without his being completely aware of them and to himself he seems to be outside his body. Without really registering what is being said he hears a conversation beside his bed about the disease which is killing him — consumption of the back and spine. His only concern in his moments of lucidity is whether the spire still stands; he is always reassured by Father Adam.

When he thinks about his death he sends for the dumb man who is to carve for his tomb a recumbent effigy of the Dean stripped of clothing and flesh. Then Jocelin drifts away again. At one point the last rites are administered but he does not die; instead he wakes in panic to full consciousness of the evil within him. He calls out for Roger Mason, hoping that at least he can be at peace with Roger again. It is Rachel, however, who arrives, bitter and angry, to tell him that Roger has tried unsuccessfully to hang himself; in the attempt he has suffered brain damage and is now blind and dumb so that she has to do everything for him. As she rails at Jocelin, Father Adam pulls her away; in Jocelin's mind she dissolves into Roger, into Goody and her childhood friends, into Pangall lying dead beneath the crossways, into the platforms of the tower from which the weight of the spire is transferred to his own back once more.

He knows the hour of his death is approaching but as he looks up he sees, not heaven, but Goody Pangall's red hair 'blazing among the stars' with his spire raised towards her. It is a sexual, not a spiritual vision but Father Adam misunderstands his scarcely audible murmur and Jocelin allows him to do so. Now he struggles and gasps in his death throes, yet he is unable to acknowledge a belief in God; he feels that heaven will be worthless unless he can take Goody Pangall and Roger there with him. He is lifted to an upright position so that he can see the spire through his window and Father Adam prepares again to administer the last rites. As he is asked for a gesture of assent to his belief in order to receive final absolution, Jocelin murmurs words about the appletree; Father Adam charitably accepts the tremor of his lips as a cry to God. Jocelin is already dead when the Host is laid upon his tongue.

Like his life, Jocelin's death leaves everything in a state of uncertainty. He dies in terror and joy. Father Adam gives him the final absolution which should allow him to enter heaven but Jocelin does not want heaven except on his own terms; these include the unlikely, the impossible salvation of Goody Pangall and Roger Mason. At the end, the spire still stands, our earlier questions unanswered.

NOTES AND GLOSSARY:

poppy: the juice from the poppy is a narcotic which was widely used in olden days to relieve pain and induce sleepiness; opium is produced from the white-flowered opium poppy

Berenice: (1) Jocelin refers to the classical myth of Berenice who dedicated herself to her husband's safe return from the wars; when she was killed by her own son her hair was said to have become the constellation

Coma Berenices. (2) Father Adam, on the other hand, thinks that Jocelin is invoking the name of the third-century Saint Berenice who was martyred in Mesopotamia in 304 AD

tap three times ... with the silver hammer: this is a reference to a ceremony performed at the death of a pope. When a pope dies they tap him on the forehead three times with a silver hammer to make sure that he is really dead

Our very stones cry out: see the Bible, Luke 19: 40, 'I tell you that, if these should hold their peace, the stones would immediately cry out.'

Part 3

Commentary

Sources for *The Spire* ?

Here, as in his earlier novels, Golding makes curious and enigmatic use of various source materials. The most immediate literary connections are with two of Ibsen's plays, *The Master Builder* (1892) and the poetic drama *Brand* (1866), both of which are concerned with obsessive aspirations to build towers and spires. Like Jocelin, Halvard Solness, Ibsen's master builder, and Pastor Brand are spurred onward by mystic visions and experiences and, like him, they both perish when their dream is accomplished. Jocelin resembles to some extent both Solness and Brand for, like the former, his vision is blurred by his frustrated sexual urge and, like the latter, he pursues to its end what may well be a satanic delusion, regardless of the cost in human misery and destruction. Golding, however, has used a number of other literary sources, creating complicated layers of reference within the novel.

The gang of vulgar labourers who are constructing the church in T.S. Eliot's early pageant play, *The Rock* (1934), may be seen as the precursors of Roger Mason's 'army'; likewise, there are affinities between Robert Browning's sixteenth-century Bishop in 'The Bishop orders his Tomb at St Praxed's Church' (1845) and Jocelin*; or, again, George Bernard Shaw's *St Joan* (1923) recalls aspects of Jocelin's vision; Joan believes that she is fulfilling the will of God presented to her through the voices of the Saints Catherine and Margaret and she pursues her obsession without counting the cost. The other significant source materials are the Bible, *The Book of Common Prayer* (or the actual rites and ceremonies of the Church) and Salisbury Cathedral itself.

For some years whilst he was a teacher at Bishop Wordsworth's School, Golding was constantly in the presence of what is generally acknowledged to be one of the most beautiful of the early English cathedrals. In the 'Visitors' Guide' to Salisbury Cathedral † Canon A.F. Smethurst asserts that it 'symbolises the peaceful loveliness of the

---

* For a fuller discussion of Golding's use of these sources see Bernard Oldsey and Stanley Weintraub, *The Art of William Golding*, Chapter 6.

† Published in the series *Pitkin Pictorial Guides and Souvenir Books*, Pitkin Pictorials, London.

English countryside amidst which it stands, the eternal truths of the
Christian Faith expressed in stone, and the continuing worship of
Almighty God'. The physical shape of the cathedral in *The Spire* is
essentially that of Salisbury; as Jocelin moves about the precincts his
steps can be traced on the plan of Salisbury; the cloisters and the Chapter
House are in identical positions and the Lady Chapel at the east end is
Salisbury's Trinity Chapel, more popularly known as the Lady Chapel.
Many of the other references, for instance those to the stone carving of
Abraham and Isaac or to the grisaille glass, both in Chapter One, are
taken directly from Salisbury. More significantly, however, when Salisbury Cathedral was built in the thirteenth century it had no spire; it was
only some hundred years later in the mid-fourteenth century that the
spire was added, despite the lack of foundations and the marshy sub-
soil. 'Perhaps', comments the Very Reverend William Fenton, some-
time Dean of Salisbury, 'the old builders just put their trust in God.'*

It is exactly this kind of remark that provides Golding with his fod-
der. Just as in *Lord of the Flies* he debunks romantic adventure stories
for boys and suggests what he believes would happen if a group of boys
became castaways on a desert island, so in *The Spire* he re-enacts a very
different kind of building exercise from that envisaged in the remark
above. *The Spire*, then, is virtually Golding's imagined account of the
building of Salisbury's spire.

The building workers of the novel are an ordinary gang of labourers
under the control of Roger Mason, the master builder. They have not
been chosen because of their piety but because they are Roger's men
and are experienced in working in wood and stone and creating great
church buildings; but they are rough men who work hard, drink hard
and swear hard. The peripatetic nature of their labour means that they
have no permanent homes and are herded together in somewhat bestial
conditions to eat and sleep wherever they are working. Jocelin's spire
gives them employment; they are paid – probably a miserable pittance
– for what they are doing but they owe Jocelin, the cathedral and God
no special allegiance. Their religion is prompted by fear and superstition so that the Christian God whose great cathedral they are building
is for them only one of a number of deities that need to be placated;
thus they follow pagan customs at the time of pagan festivals as a kind
of insurance policy against the possibility of thunderbolts.

Evil and sin are rife. Life is held of little account; men die horribly in
the course of the work, are attacked and killed in quarrels or, like Pangall, are sacrificed in heathen rites. The master builder commits adultery with the caretaker's wife under the very eye of God within the
cathedral and both the resulting baby and Goody Pangall herself die in

---

* See *AA Hand-picked Tours in Britain*, Drive Publications, Basingstoke, 1977, p.54.

childbirth. The latent animosities among the cathedral clergy rise to the surface and Jocelin's own life is finally destroyed by his dedication to the building. Somewhere along the way Golding's account has vastly diverged from the accepted belief of the spire built by faith.

From the Bible are taken the threads of many stories, the most significant of these, because of its importance in Golding's work as a whole, is the story of the Fall (Genesis, 3). Yet references to this story do not become overt until the penultimate chapter when Anselm paraphrases words from Genesis 3 in blaming Jocelin for the loss of his (Anselm's) integrity: 'You tempted me and I did eat.' The biblical fall from Grace in the Old Testament is followed by Christ's sacrifice and God's forgiveness in the New Testament, but Anselm proves himself unable to forgive; from that moment, however, Jocelin's mind seems to dwell on the Fall and the need for forgiveness. When he escapes from the Deanery and the watchful eye of Father Adam in order to seek out Roger Mason and ask forgiveness of him, the first thing Jocelin sees is an appletree in full bloom with what appears to be a snake in its branches.* In that instant he understands the extent of Man's responsibility for evil: the appletree had other branches, not corrupted by sin and temptation, but Jocelin had chosen to respond to the 'long black springing thing' hidden in the midst of the innocence of the apple blossom – the serpent, the witches' broom of the mistletoe, the phallus. Coming at this stage in the novel, the references to the Fall demand a re-assessment on the part of the reader of all that has gone before.

The theme of temptation is rooted in yet another biblical story, this time Satan's temptation of Jesus (Matthew 4: 1–11). As Jocelin climbs up the scaffolding in Chapter Five he is compared to a boy climbing 'too high in a forbidden tree' (an earlier if less obvious reference to the Fall). At the top he is aware of sin: 'Pangall at the broom's end, one of the army dancing towards him, the spire projecting obscenely between his legs. He saw a fall of red hair.' At the top of the high mountain and on the pinnacle of the temple Jesus resisted the temptations to power and self-glory but Jocelin succumbs to them, rejoicing in his position, wishing the spire to be a thousand feet high so that he could 'oversee the whole country'. It is from the top of the tower one day that he hears Roger Mason mutter, 'I believe you're the devil. The devil himself' (Chapter Six).

The story of the Tower of Babel (Genesis 11: 1–9) also seems to have some relevance as a source, for not only is it one of the earliest recorded tower stories but also it resulted in men's language being confounded so that they were unable to communicate with each other. Certainly,

---

* It is not quite the classic picture of the Fall of Eve, for Jocelin's appletree is in blossom, not in fruit.

the higher Jocelin's spire rises, the more difficult he finds it to make any genuine point of contact with others. Apart from these stories there are innumerable echoes and references to the Bible, most of which have a significance far beyond their simple contextual one.

There are, too, many references to the services of the Church, with quotations taken from *The Book of Common Prayer*; there is a double anachronism embodied in this, for not only does *The Book of Common Prayer* belong to the Anglican Church but also it was not in existence in the fourteenth century. However, by its use Golding is able to evoke certain responses from his readers which could not have been obtained by anything less than a standard reference. In the first chapter the Creed is used subtly to introduce the theme of sin and judgement which overlays Jocelin's attitude to his aunt Alison, the King's mistress. As her letter is read aloud by Father Adam the chanting of the Creed from the service being conducted in the Lady Chapel impinges itself upon Jocelin's consciousness as a sort of commentary upon her words; such phrases as 'those faults I still find it so difficult entirely to repent of' are followed by the chanted 'The forgiveness of sins and the life everlasting'. There are many other Prayer Book quotations and allusions in the novel but none is used so consistently as this.

Golding's use of sources is never simple. By exploiting a number of source works, none of them followed through to their original conclusions, he is able to achieve slight shifts in perspective which allow the reader to see the action in varying lights. Like all his other novels, *The Spire* is rooted in many earlier works but finally it resembles none.

Narrative form and voice

The Spire is ostensibly a third-person narrative but it is not told by an omniscient narrator. Until the last short paragraph the whole story is filtered to us through the consciousness of Dean Jocelin. There is no objective narration; Jocelin is continuously present throughout the whole novel, violently, ecstatically alive on the opening page and dead in the last few words. The novel never progresses without him, nor sidesteps to follow the fortunes of others. Our view of events is given us entirely through his eyes and we see other characters as he sees them and as they present themselves to him. What he does not see we are unable to see; thus, when Pangall is driven to his death, we do not at first know what has happened to him and are even ready to accept Father Adam's version of events: 'As for . . . Pangall; he's run away' (Chapter Five). Yet later we are able to accept with complete conviction the picture of pagan sacrifice that Jocelin has by then come to believe: 'poor Pangall, crouched beneath the crossways, with a sliver of mistletoe between his ribs' (Chapter Eleven). Likewise, the progression of the passionate affair between Goody and Roger is entirely hidden from us until Jocelin comes upon them in the swallow's nest (Chapter Six).

Golding has complicated the narrative form, however, by presenting us with various levels of Jocelin's conscious and unconscious mind. We are thus able to deduce things of which Jocelin himself is apparently unaware. We know that Pangall is dead long before Jocelin knows; we realise that Goody is bearing Roger's child before Jocelin hears them together in the swallow's nest; moreover, our understanding of Jocelin's physical desire for Goody is earthy and realistic, though he tells even himself that he loves her as his 'daughter in God'. These dual views of events are made possible by the subtlety of Golding's language and presentation. At times the story progresses on one plane whilst an apparently arbitrary juxtaposition of events introduces an objective commentary on it; the chanting of the Creed in Chapter One is a simple instance of this. A similar narrative device, though different in kind and far more complicated, is employed in Chapter Four when Roger tries to persuade Jocelin to abandon the building of the spire: on one level, the ordinary conscious one, Jocelin conducts a straightforward discussion with Roger; on another level, still conscious, he is a hunter, stalking and finally trapping an animal; on a third level, suppressed, almost subconscious, is his understanding of what he is committing Roger and Goody to in keeping the master builder at the cathedral; yet, when Roger shouts, 'You just don't know what'll come out of our going on!' it is not entirely true; Jocelin has counted – but miscalculated – the cost.

There are some disadvantages in this very subjective method of narration, particularly in that the form itself is deceptive: whilst appearing to be a third-person account and therefore, to some extent at least, objective, it is more akin to a biased first-person account; Jocelin's view of himself and of others is by no means accurate, but it takes the reader some while to come to terms with the truth. Father Adam, for instance, he re-names 'Father Anonymous' because he sees him as faceless and easily forgettable, but finally it is Father Adam who stays in our mind as being the most loyal, the most 'Christian', the best of the Fathers. Our view of Anselm's intransigence, too, is based on Jocelin's account of his long-standing friendship with the old man: 'he remembered how thick and long the thread had been, a rope binding them heart to heart' (Chapter Two). It is not until Chapter Eleven that we find ourselves forced to revise this view; Jocelin may have seen Anselm as his oldest friend but Anselm's memories are different: 'You were all over my knees like a dog'; 'Why must you always have a very best friend, like an ignorant girl?'; 'Why was I the object of this – adolescent regard?' Additionally, when Jocelin becomes incoherent towards the end of the novel it is very difficult for the reader to follow what is happening.

On the other hand, one of Golding's most effective narrative devices in this novel is based upon these 'disadvantages'; he intends us to see events and people in a continually shifting perspective and, though the story is filtered through Jocelin's consciousness, in the end we are by no means limited to Jocelin's point of view.

Golding's narrative method in *The Spire* should not be seen as a 'stream-of-consciousness' method, for the story, the actual events, not the mind of Jocelin, direct the progress of the novel. It is a method that Golding has used in other novels and has made peculiarly – and successfully – his own.

The spiritual dimension

Though *The Spire* is a story about the building of a cathedral spire, the underlying theme is concerned with the nature of Evil. The novel begins in glory and light in the presence of 'God the Father'. Dean Jocelin is full of joy and love; three times in the early pages of the first chapter he is depicted as feeling love – in the sense of holy love – first for the ancient chancellor, next for Goody Pangall and then for the two young deacons. A less happy note soon creeps in, however: the two deacons are indulging in unkind gossip; Pangall is distressed and afraid; a man has been killed by Roger Mason's labourers; Jocelin is annoyed and irritated with Pangall and does not offer him any real comfort; nor, despite his office, does he extend any love or forgiveness to his elderly but erring aunt Alison.

Yet these are merely venial sins and do not call into question the nature of faith or of good and evil. The real problems are concerned with the truth of Jocelin's vision and the apparent miracle of the spire. Jocelin himself asserts that he was chosen by God to plan the spire and that Roger was chosen 'to fill the diagram with glass and iron and stone' (Chapter Six). His arguments appear convincing as he explains to Roger:

> Even in the old days [God] never asked men to do what was reasonable. Men can do that for themselves. They can buy and sell, heal and govern. But then out of some deep place comes the command to do what makes no sense at all... Then, if men have faith, a new thing comes.

> (Chapter Six)

Furthermore, Jocelin believes that he has been specifically favoured by God and that his own personal angel visits and comforts him regularly. The proof of his conviction appears to be that, despite the lack of foundations and Roger's belief that the pillars will not stand the weight, the spire is built and still stands at the end of the novel. By that point, however, inspiration and faith have become tarnished. The comforting warmth of the visiting angel proves to be an early sign of the crippling spinal disease which finally destroys Jocelin; even on a mystic plane the visitations cannot be seen as those of an angel who ultimately becomes an avenging angel, for when Jocelin is struck down with 'a whitehot flail' it is by a fallen angel, a devil with 'cloven hoof' (Chapter Ten). Then, late in the story, we learn that God's chosen priest Jocelin became Dean of the cathedral, not through his own obvious superiority, piety and holiness, but through the patronage, the nepotism of his aunt and her lover, the dissolute King.

What then of the vision? What of the spire itself? If the comforting angel has all along been the devil in disguise, may not the spire also be held up by Satan? May the miracle not be Jocelin's reward for doing Satan's work? The allegory of angels and devils is appropriate to the medieval setting but it also points to the very real problems of good and evil and Man's struggle to come to terms with them. Jocelin believes at first in his own goodness and innocence but he has not counted the true cost of the tower: one by one he sacrifices to the work those he has held dear: he sacrifices his friendship with Anselm, the purity of Goody Pangall, Pangall's life, the integrity of Roger Mason and his own peace of mind. Step by step, however, he is led to an understanding of the nature of Evil, to a knowledge that he had suppressed for the sake of realising his ambition to build the spire. 'I didn't know how much you would cost up there' he cries out after the thread of his friendship with Anselm has been snapped (Chapter Two). 'I didn't know' follows his interview with Pangall and Pangall's bitterness in Chapter Three; after his agonised decision to allow Goody to be sacrificed he prays to his angel, 'I need you! Before today I didn't really know why' (Chapter Three).

Even in the myth of the Fall it is the *knowledge* that produces Evil; when Eve ate the apple from the Tree of the Knowledge of Good and Evil it was not merely the fact that she disobeyed that brought about the Fall but the simultaneous revelation that she *knew* she had done wrong. *The Spire* is, throughout, concerned with Jocelin's growing awareness of his will to wrongdoing. 'Oh the lessons I have learned', he thinks to himself when he hears that Goody Pangall is pregnant and, in the moment of terror during her labour, he prays 'have mercy, I didn't know it was to be this'. It is not until the end of Chapter Nine, however, that full understanding comes to him as he sinks into a sexual dream which, for a brief while, brings him peace of a kind. As he comes to himself at the beginning of Chapter Ten we are told that 'he was left, helplessly in the grip of the new knowledge'. It is the turning-point of the novel. Until that moment Jocelin has not grasped the significance of the knowledge he is acquiring; after that he begins to realise that the will to evil comes from within himself and is not ordained by God in order that good may come. He has been searching vainly for someone to blame; even after this he still tries to avoid the responsibility by blaming his evil desires on witchcraft, on Goody, on Roger; but, finally, he knows that he had the choice; he could have chosen Good and not Evil; he could have saved Pangall and Goody and Roger by sacrificing his own ambition to build the spire. In saving them he could have saved himself from the torment of prurient thoughts and the haunting presence of the dead Goody.

At the end, however, the spire still stands, and as Jocelin views it through the window of his death-chamber he is moved with terror and joy; it is both fearful and beautiful; like the appletree it embodies both Good and Evil, so that in the moment of death he feels that he knows nothing except that Man has a choice and thus that evil is not outside Man but is within him.

From the last paragraph we may deduce what we will; it appears to suggest comfort after agony, to offer to Jocelin the final hope of redemption.

The sexual dimension

The spire as phallic symbol is made very obvious in this novel from an early stage. Jocelin himself, as he looks at the model of the cathedral, delineates the idea in a comparison, of the significance of which only he is innocent:

> The model was like a man lying on his back. The nave was his legs placed together, the transepts on either side were his arms outspread. The choir was his body; and the Lady Chapel ... was his head. And now, also, springing, projecting, bursting, erupting from the heart of the building, there was its crown and majesty, the new spire.
>
> (Chapter One)

Certainly the labourers are swift to take advantage of the vulgar opportunity put at their disposal, using the model spire to torment the lame and fearful Pangall.

However, just as the spire dominates the story on one plane, so does the phallus dominate it on another. Jocelin's problem is not merely that he wishes above all else to build a cathedral spire which penetrates the purity of the sky, but that he also desires (though the desire is deep, deep within his unconscious) to use his own rich and burgeoning spire to penetrate his 'daughter in God'. As a Catholic priest he is unable to marry and should remain celibate. The passion conceived in his young manhood for the child who has become Goody Pangall has long been concealed in the guise of the holy love a pastor should feel for those in his care; but Jocelin has tried to preserve her from the taint of worldly love, to maintain her virginity and keep her inviolate, by an arranged marriage with the impotent Pangall; only thus is he able to keep his prurient imagination at bay, for her virgin purity protects her, even from the lewdness of thought. It provides security for Jocelin, too, for while she is Pangall's wife he can escape the pangs of jealousy: she is not his, but neither is she Pangall's, except in name.

Goody's entanglement with the virile Roger makes Jocelin fear the loss of her purity and thus the loss of his sexual immunity; he is tormented and tortured by his imagination. Worse, however, her defection comes at a time when Jocelin realises its value to boost his other obsession, the building of the spire. He finds himself in a spiritual and sexual dilemma: if, as priest and Dean of the Cathedral, he intervenes and the affair comes to an end, he may achieve both spiritual and sexual peace again but Roger may refuse to go on with the precarious building project and Jocelin will have no hold on him; if, on the other hand, he abdicates his priestly duty and allows the liaison to continue, Roger is sure to stay. The terrible thought springs into his mind, 'She will keep him here.' These five monosyllabic words, standing alone on the page with space all around them, indicate the end of Jocelin's struggle with his conscience and the weightiness of the decision he makes; they are the sign of his capitulation; he will sacrifice Goody and his own peace of mind for the sake of his vision.

Immediately after he observes the attraction exercised over Goody Pangall by Roger, Jocelin has an encounter with Rachel Mason in which she talks with 'gross impropriety' about her sexual problems; his horror and indignation at this indelicate confidence rouses, however, his sexual appetites; in his disturbed and impassioned state of mind he has a sudden erection which torments him.

From now on his two obsessions run parallel with each other; as the spire grows, so do Jocelin's sexual needs, yet he will not allow the one to stop, though it would help to still the other; 'now there was a kind of necessary marriage', we are told, 'Jocelin, and the spire' (Chapter Five). He is haunted by Goody Pangall's red hair and confuses her in his mind with Gilbert the dumb man, his 'son in God', for Gilbert is devoted to the Dean and is 'like a good dog' (Chapter Five), a state of mind he can never expect from Goody.

Goody's death in the horror of an abortive childbirth, surrounded by blood, does nothing to release him from his sexual turmoil but, rather, increases it until he is almost demented. However, only with the completion of the spire, after the Holy Nail has been beaten into it, does Jocelin reach his sexual climax in the phantom arms of Goody Pangall (Chapter Nine). It is a moment of respite which eases him but does not end his agony, for the carnal knowledge which his orgasm brings him releases his body but not his mind. He still has to understand the extent of his own responsibility; he blames the devil, he blames witchcraft, he blames Goody and Roger for coming 'so flatly between [him] and heaven' (Chapter Ten).

The last three chapters are confused because Jocelin's mind is confused. Sex and spirituality are inextricably mingled in his thoughts, just as the mistletoe and the appletree, symbols respectively of pagan abandon and Christian doctrine, are entangled with each other. His final hours appear to culminate in doubts as to whether his adherence to his religion is more meaningful to him than human understanding and friendship. When he visits Roger he lays aside his priesthood – his cloak, his skullcap and his cross; he ponders about 'some mode of life where all love is good, where one love can't compete with another but adds to it' (Chapter Eleven). He cannot conceive of heaven, if it is a heaven without Roger and Goody; he comes to realise that he sacrificed them, not for human love, but for a religious concept, the cathedral spire, the great phallic symbol pointing toward heaven. Thus, in the moment of death, when he feels that assent to belief is being wrenched from him, he clings to that other symbol – the symbol of choice – the appletree which holds the possibility of salvation or damnation and leaves the choice to him.

Characters

Roger's army

Though the action of *The Spire* involves a good part of the medieval community in a small cathedral town, few of them are differentiated. They are seen almost entirely through the eyes of Dean Jocelin, the only exception to this being when one character speaks of another; even then it is in Jocelin's presence and generally in words spoken to him. Roger Mason's 'army' of workmen, though during the course of the novel they perform the prodigious task of building the spire, remain as little more than background to the story. We know few of their names: Jehan is Roger's assistant and second-in-command who takes over the day-to-day organisation of the work when Roger himself withdraws; Ranulf is small and wizened but a hard-working, steady man who, when he realises how precarious the building is, becomes disaffected, packs up his tools and leaves; one of Roger's 'best stonecutters' (not even named) is killed in a brawl. Apart from these the workmen have no individual or distinguishing characteristics. As a group they are a rough, uncouth lot: they have no respect for the place they are working in and little for the cathedral dignitaries around them. They drink, swear, sing bawdy songs, quarrel, fight, even commit murder; in the midst of it all they work hard; under Roger's guidance they work skilfully and it is through them that Jocelin's ambition – the spire – is achieved.

Their very physical presence throughout the novel, however, serves the purpose of suggesting the confusion and chaos which the building work has brought to the cathedral; they are omnipresent, covering the sacred precincts with dust, stone-chippings, wood-shavings, glass-slithers, mocking at Pangall, deriding Roger and Rachel, first laughing at, then tolerating and finally welcoming the Dean. This amorphous group of men give atmosphere to the novel more effectively than had Golding presented them through a small, selected number of more clearly delineated individuals.

Jocelin

We are given little physical description of Jocelin except that we know he is a tall man; reference is made to his height a number of times in the first chapter: as he bows 'his skullcapped head' to pass through the little door from the south transept to the yard, Pangall is 'under his left shoulder' and a moment after we are told that Pangall's head was 'six inches below Jocelin's face'. Later, whilst he talks to the dumb man, we get an inkling of the reason for emphasis being put upon his height: he is proud of his physical appearance and clearly delighted that he has been chosen as model for the gargoyles representing flying angels which are to be built into the tower two hundred feet up. When in Chapter Eight Jocelin examines his reflection in Roger's polished metal sheet we realise the physical toll that has been taken of him by the events that have passed; but even this is not the worst for, on his last excursion outside to see Roger, he is scarcely able to walk; he is 'bent nearly double' and 'like an old crow' (Chapter Eleven).

Likewise, we are provided with few biographical facts about him: though his mother was pious, his aunt Alison became a courtesan, the King's mistress, a sin which Jocelin finds it hard to forgive. As a young man he entered a monastery as a novice and there he met Anselm, father of the novices, to whom he became devoted. When, suddenly, he found himself rising through the hierarchy of the Church – deacon, priest, dean – he believed it was owing to his own worth; in his pride he persuaded Anselm to come to the cathedral as Sacrist; only in his final interview with Alison do we realise that his promotion did not indicate his own merit but arose from an act of nepotism, almost a practical joke on the part of his aunt and her lover, the King.

Despite the paucity of background description, however, Jocelin is the most significant character in the novel. We see the whole story through his eyes and we follow his spiritual journey from innocence to knowledge, from ignorance to understanding. He is an equivocal figure, holy man and sinner, to some a type of Christ, to others a sort of devil. Jocelin is a man obsessed by an ambition. He believes that he has been chosen by God to bring a new glory to the cathedral, to raise a spire and himself to be raised, 'resurrected from daily life' (Chapter Ten) into a oneness with God, 'an implacable, unstoppable, glorious fountain of the spirit, a wild burning of me for Thee' (Chapter Ten). By the time the action of the novel begins he has so fully identified himself with the spire that its erection has become necessary to his personal fulfilment.

When considering Jocelin's character it is as irrelevant to wonder whether his 'vision' is genuine as to be concerned whether his rise in the Church by irregular means has in some way damaged him spiritually. It is enough to know that he himself is not handicapped by these doubts, for they do not arise until after the spire has been completed. Bowing to the overriding demand on his attention, he suppresses and consigns to the 'cellerage' of his mind all thoughts that might impede the progress of the building. He appears to be, conventionally, a 'good' man: he cares about God's House; he spends time in prayer; he radiates love to those around him. However, in the first two chapters he meets with several challenges and he fails them all: in his irritation and impatience he fails to dispense comfort to Pangall; he fails to extend forgiveness or to show Christian charity to his aunt Alison and he displays anger and selfishness towards Father Anselm, his confessor and teacher. We are thus prepared for his much greater dereliction of duty in Chapter Three when he first observes the attraction between Goody Pangall and Roger Mason. This arouses passions in him that he has been unaware of; anger, jealousy, prurience overwhelm him and, even as he prays for Goody, a more evil thought enters his mind: he will make use of the illicit affair to keep Roger at work on the spire. One by one he sacrifices to his obsession those whom he has held dear and those who depend on him — Anselm, Pangall, Goody and Roger; yet he continues to deceive himself into accepting that God demands the sacrifices: 'If they are part of the cost, why so be it', he tells himself in Chapter Five.

Jocelin, however, bears within himself the seeds of his own destruction; the wasting 'consumption of the back and spine' (Chapter Twelve) from which he dies destroys him physically but it is the evil which festers in his own soul that destroys him spiritually. He has both pandered to and failed to recognise his own sexual feelings for Goody; in arranging her marriage to Pangall, however, he has not only kept her for himself but he has deprived her of fulfilment; in surrendering her to Roger he has submitted himself to sexual agony and her to an illicit relationship which torments and finally kills her. Only when the spire is complete and the Holy Nail has been driven home is Jocelin made aware of the fragility of his dream – the pillars which support the whole edifice are not of solid stone but are stone skins, filled with rubble and rubbish. The allegory is now complete: the spire appears to be built, like his own chastity, on a lie and a deception. He is at last forced to acknowledge his own guilt, to offer not others but himself as a sacrifice: 'I have given it my back' (Chapter Ten).

In the last two chapters Jocelin moves towards expiation: he puts aside the symbols of his priesthood and begs Roger for human forgiveness. Spiritually, he is no longer certain of anything; humanly, he has travelled a long way, for he is now aware that he tried to use others to advance his own spiritual standing and he is ready to reject the final reward in exchange for human companionship: 'what is heaven to me unless I go in holding him by one hand and her by the other?' (Chapter Twelve). At his death he finally affirms his belief in humankind, '*It's like the appletree!*' – Man is Man because he has the knowledge of Good and Evil.

Roger Mason

Though Jocelin is the inspiration behind the building of the spire, the skill and ability to fulfil the vision are Roger Mason's. He is a strong, stocky, powerful man with dark skin and close-cropped head; at various times in the novel he is described as a bull and a bear and Jocelin thinks of him as 'Bullet Head'. His superlative skill and technical knowledge have won him fame and without him Jocelin knows that the spire will never be finished: 'There's no one but you who can build it. That's what they said. Notable Roger Mason' (Chapter Four).

When we first meet him Roger is a tough, taciturn man, but, married to a garrulous wife, he has avoided all the bawdy sexual involvements of his own army. He is a leader, keeping his men together, providing work for them, caring for them in his own way just as Jocelin should be caring for the congregation in his charge. Thus, Roger appears, at bottom, to be a good man until he sees Goody Pangall. Then he becomes helpless, drawn by some magnetic power that is greater than himself, 'as though nothing and no one in the whole world mattered, as though he could not help her mattering and was tormented by her mattering' (Chapter Three). A more worldly man than Jocelin, Roger is aware of the insidious strength of sexual attraction; he tries to resist it but the affair flourishes, though for several months, since we see only through Jocelin's eyes, we do not know how far it has advanced. Using the instability of the building work as an excuse, Roger tries to extricate himself and go away before things have progressed too far, but Jocelin traps him there. Only much later (in Chapter Eleven) do we understand that, following this entrapment, Roger at least connives in, if he does not actually arrange, the ritual murder of his helpless rival, Pangall.

After Goody's death Roger is a broken man; he returns to his wife, not so much as a loving husband but as, metaphorically, her captive slave (Chapter Eight). Doubly a prisoner, Roger turns to drink, ceases to take an interest in his work, neglects his men and becomes thoroughly debauched. Yet, at his last meeting with Jocelin the inherent goodness in him briefly surfaces: unlike Father Anselm, he is ready to offer free, sincere and compassionate forgiveness to the man who has destroyed him, though his good impulse does not last long. He is a pathetic figure at the end, sitting 'by the fire, his head on one side, blind and dumb ... Like a baby' (Chapter Twelve).

Goody Pangall

Goody Pangall may be seen as Jocelin's principal victim. A pretty, red-haired child, whose father worked in the precincts of the cathedral, she had attracted Jocelin's attention as she skipped and danced with her playmates. He found himself drawn to her and, though he did not admit it even to himself, his feelings for her were not those of holy love but of sexual lust. To quieten them and to save himself the pangs of jealousy, he arranged her marriage to an impotent man, the small lame son of another cathedral worker. Thus, Goody is deprived of any genuine sexual fulfilment within her marriage.

When Roger, in his turn, is attracted to her she responds to him passionately, drawn, despite herself, into a web of intrigue, trapped in what Jocelin sees as a 'tent that shut them off from all other people' (Chapter Three). She clearly is sexually attractive and, as a child, may have been a bit of a coquette, but there is no suggestion that she is in any way a loose woman. Her struggles to escape entanglement with Roger are hinted at when Jocelin first sees them together; she shrinks from the master builder and appears to reject his advances, yet finally the two of them are enmeshed.

Though she plays a major part in the novel, we know remarkably little about Goody; we do not know her real name, how she occupies her day, or her feelings towards her husband. When, at the end of the novel, Jocelin tries to re-assess events he is tormented by the thought that Goody may have connived in Pangall's murder. Though we do not suspect a sin so heinous, we recognise that, unlike Jocelin, she saw and understood what had happened to her husband. Her death in childbirth, terrible though it is, releases her from her agonies and anxieties.

Pangall

Pangall is the cathedral caretaker. His family's connection with the cathedral goes back a hundred and fifty years to the time when his great-great-grandfather helped to build it and later saved it from burning down.

Pangall himself is a small man with a lame left foot and a slightly mad expression on his face ('the raging look' – Chapter Two). He knows himself to be impotent, but, married to a pretty woman, he tries to make the best of the situation. He is devoted to his work and dreams that one day he, like his ancestor, will save the cathedral from destruction. Instead he now sees the confusion and mess and feels that the place is being destroyed before his eyes. Moreover, within the very precincts of the cathedral which he holds dear he finds himself mocked, jeered at and struck by newcomers who care nothing for the sanctity of the place. When he turns to the Dean for comfort and spiritual solace he receives none but is told, 'You're too thinskinned, man. You must put up with it' (Chapter One).

Despite, or perhaps because of, his physical disabilities he is a sensitive man: puzzled and distressed at the disruption of his daily routine he pleads for understanding and weeps for his own inadequacies. Yet when he is talking of the cathedral he displays a fervour which expresses itself in an almost poetic and certainly an evocative turn of phrase: 'When snow falls and all that weight lies on the lead roof; when leaves choke the gutter', or again, 'He made a hole you could hide a, a child in; and he carried the embers out in arms that were roasted like pork' (Chapter One). His hesitancy here, when he thinks of a child, is an indication of his sadness, perhaps bitterness, in the face of his own impotence. He shows, too, an understanding and sensitivity that Jocelin does not appear to credit him with, for when the Dean ineptly talks to him of his sons rejoicing in the work done in their father's time (Chapter Three), Pangall feels that he is being taunted and limps away.

His disappearance and death do not surprise us; he is no match for the rough and tough labourers when they attack him and, like Simon in *Lord of the Flies*, his abnormalities make him a natural victim; the desire to destroy what is odd, what is different and therefore not fully understood develops into 'the hunting noise of the pack' (Chapter Four) and ends in Pangall's death as a sacrifice to pagan gods to ward off bad luck. Thus, he is built into the foundations and becomes part of the cathedral he loves.

Rachel Mason

Rachel is a minor character but she is the fourth of the pillars which prop up Jocelin's spire and the fourth of his main victims. 'I traded a stone hammer for four people' he remarks in Chapter Twelve. A loud-mouthed, gossiping woman, she is not very attractive. It is, however, the building of the spire which destroys her life. She and Roger have always been devoted to each other, 'revolving round each other' (Chapter Two) and no scandal has ever touched them. When she learns of Roger's association with Goody she is furiously angry and re-asserts her marital rights by dragging Roger away from Pangall's cottage, haranguing and beating him.

After Goody's death Roger and Rachel return to each other but she now acts like a jealous wife, watching over him and allowing him no freedom to betray her again. Yet, she appears, despite everything, genuinely to love her husband. His attempted suicide after Jocelin's visit to him leaves her miserable and distraught.

Father Anselm

Father Anselm, who is one of the Principal Persons at the Cathedral, is Jocelin's oldest acquaintance; they had first met when Jocelin was a novice and Anselm the master of the novices in a monastery by the sea. Their long acquaintanceship has been marked by strong affection on Jocelin's side but this has not been sincerely reciprocated by Anselm; he was originally 'Amused and touched. And irritated' (Chapter Eleven). He, nevertheless, accepted Jocelin's hand of friendship and the promotion which came with it when, after he became Dean, Jocelin asked his old master to serve as Sacrist at the cathedral and to be his Confessor. Anselm is, however, envious of Jocelin's rise: the younger man not only overtook him through a shabby and sinful patronage but, to add insult to injury, the patron died before any real power could be conferred on either of them. Thus they stagnated there in their positions until Jocelin gave himself spurious fame through the building of the cathedral spire, an act which Anselm opposed in the Chapter.

When we first see Anselm it is Jocelin who appears to be disadvantaged in our eyes. The Sacrist has been appointed to guard the nave and ensure that the sanctity of the cathedral is as little disturbed as possible while the work progresses. The stone dust in the old man's lungs, however, has forced him to abandon his watch and go out into the fresh air in the square within the cloisters; meanwhile, Jocelin is angered by hearing one of the labourers within the cathedral singing a bawdy song and realises that there is no one on watch. Anselm comes well out of the slightly acrimonious exchange which follows for he appears to display Christian charity, refusing to 'ask others to do what I can't do myself' (Chapter Two). On the other hand, we should notice that when Jocelin tries to patch up the quarrel it is Anselm who refuses to meet him halfway.

Anselm is both petty and vindictive. He is angry because the work on the spire prevents him from carrying out his lucrative trade of selling candles to burn at the altars of the cathedral; he also secretly makes a number of reports to his superiors, complaining about Jocelin. As the story progresses we become aware of Anselm's bitter resentment against Jocelin, a resentment which, though humanly understandable, tarnishes the godly image of a Father of the Church. Even when Jocelin is dying Anselm has to be asked twice before he goes to him. In the interview at this time the Sacrist displays both selfishness and malice, rehearsing old grudges and even criticising the form of Jocelin's past confessions. When Jocelin begs forgiveness for all that he is and all that has gone before, Anselm replies perfunctorily, 'Naturally I forgive you. I forgive you' (Chapter Eleven), a reply which exudes insincerity. We feel that, for all his faults, Jocelin is, at bottom, a better man than Anselm who still refuses to accept his responsibilities.

Style and language

The complications of style and language in Golding's novels go far beyond the mere problems of vocabulary. In *The Spire* the architectural and ecclesiastical terms may initially appear to cause problems but they are fairly easily resolved through recourse to the 'Notes and Glossary' sections or to a dictionary. Likewise, the few archaic words (such as 'busyness' in Chapter One) or pseudo-medieval words (such as 'ungood' in Chapter Eight) cause little difficulty. The multi-layered pattern of the language as a whole is, however, more elusive. Even what seem to be the simplest of similes and metaphors often carry implications well beyond the original point of comparison.

The most consistent series of images is that concerned with animals. Many of these are merely descriptive – the 'bat-thin' voice of the ancient Chancellor (Chapter One), the 'mouse voice' of Father Adam (Chapter One) or the 'snail slowness' of Ranulf (Chapter Eight). Roger Mason is more than once said to be 'like a bear' and in Chapter Eight he scrambles sideways 'like a crab'; these, again, appear to be purely descriptive phrases but what do we make of the simile, used first in Chapter Two, that he is 'like a bull'? Clearly it describes his stature and his strength but it also seems to carry some sexual connotation; at one point it is associated with the word 'stallion' (Chapter Three).

Jocelin is frequently referred to in such imagery: to Anselm he is 'like a dog' (Chapter Eleven), a phrase more often applied to the dumb man; Jocelin's thoughts are 'like a horse unharnessed from the cart' (Chapter Twelve) and when in Chapter Ten he is made to see how deceptive are the supports of his spire and he finds himself physically struck down by his spinal disease, his body throws itself around 'like a broken snake', itself a two-edged simile in view of the Fall imagery in the novel. Jocelin is most often, however, compared to a bird. Early on he sees himself as an eagle (Chapter One); the power and strength in flight of the eagle appeals to him; it is also, of course, a bird of prey, its victims always being living creatures. When, after the death of Pangall, he climbs up into the tower he stands 'like a raven on the edge of a cliff' (Chapter Five), but it is in the latter part of the novel that the nobility of the eagle is lost; Jocelin is then likened to 'an old crow' (Chapter Eleven) and 'a bird caught in a window' (Chapter Twelve). On the very last page, trapped between life and death, he becomes the 'bluebird', the kingfisher he had earlier observed flashing over the river beside the deanery, an image which seems to hold out more hope than that of the scavengers with whom he has earlier been compared.

Far more difficult to follow are the various allegorical references that run through the book. The picture of the cathedral as ark or ship is introduced early in the first chapter. Jocelin there sees himself as captain, knowing exactly what his crew is doing at any given moment. Ropes and ladders lead up to the swallow's nest in the tower, just as on a sailing ship the rigging goes up to the crow's-nest observation point. When Jocelin looks around him and thinks 'There is no good thing in all this circle but the great house, the ark, the refuge, a ship to contain all these people and now fitted with a mast' (Chapter Five), it is clear that the ship for him is Noah's Ark (see the Bible, Genesis 6–8); Noah's ark for us is the place where 'the animals went in, two by two' as the old rhyme has it, which seems to put a somewhat more sinister and sexual interpretation on Jocelin's ship-image.

Though the overt references to it begin late in the novel, the most significant of all the allegorical layers is that which deals with the Fall of Man and the problem of evil. As soon as the appletree is introduced in Chapter Eleven it retrospectively pulls into focus other references which have meant less in isolation: the serpent, good and evil, heaven and hell, angels and devils, knowing and not knowing are all part of the biblical story. Viewed in this way, we may see the novel as tracing the progress of Jocelin's Fall. There is a curious short sentence near the end of Chapter Eleven when Jocelin, who has been thrown out by Roger and beaten by the mob, comes to himself: 'I am naked, he thought, that was to be expected'; the reason for the expectation can be understood only by reference to the words of Genesis 3: 10 and 11.

And [Adam] said, I heard thy voice in the garden, and I was afraid, because I was naked; and I hid myself.

And [God] said, Who told thee that thou wast naked? Hast thou eaten of the tree, whereof I commanded thee that thou shouldest not eat?

Jocelin has indeed eaten the forbidden fruit and his words are an acknowledgement that his Fall is accomplished; he has the knowledge of Good and Evil.

Interwoven with the biblical story is a complicated thread of pagan magic and witchcraft. It begins with the rotting berry which Jocelin scuffs off his shoe in Chapter Five, not long after the death of Pangall. Even Jocelin at that time does not recognise that it is mistletoe. Only much later, at the end of Chapter Eight* when the labourers have gone to join in the devil worship around the Midsummer fires, does he recall the berry and think of the connection of mistletoe with this heathen ceremony; from that point he is probably aware, at least in his subconscious, that Pangall was sacrificed in the Midsummer rites of the previous year. For us the pattern is still incomplete, for we need to know that mistletoe is a parasite which grows on certain trees and that the mistletoe most prized by the old Druid priests who initiated these ceremonies was that which grew on appletrees; further the parasitic growths of the plant on the host tree are called 'witches' brooms'. In Chapter Eleven Jocelin sees such a growth in an appletree outside the deanery; it looks to him very like a serpent; the serpent itself is both the biblical devil and a phallic symbol, introducing yet another layer of meaning into the already complicated allegory of the Fall. At the same time the strange plant which has haunted his mind is explained: it is the mistletoe, 'complex, twining, engulfing, destroying, strangling . . . a riot of foliage and flowers and overripe, bursting fruit' (Chapter Ten); and he, Jocelin, is the appletree in which 'the evil plant' (Chapter Eleven) has been growing and where the serpent has been lying hidden.

The cathedral as human body and the spire as phallus have already been glanced at in the section on 'The sexual dimension'. Jocelin's spinal disease is no coincidence; the similarity of the words 'spine' and 'spire' underlines a parallel development: as the novel progresses Jocelin feels that on his back he bears the whole weight of the physical building just as within himself he bears the moral corruption that has marred the purity of his original vision. The poppy-drugged body of the church in Chapter One on which he, as surgeon, performs the operation of carving out the belly to erect the spire, becomes in the final chapter his own broken, emasculated body, itself drugged with poppy to alleviate the pain.

The reader should investigate for himself the symbols of imprisonment and Jocelin's allegory of his own mind as a cellerage filled with rats.

In some ways the sunlight streaming through the stained-glass windows of the cathedral, the incessant, dreary, torrential rain, the consuming fog may be seen to allegorise Golding's stylistic method in this

---

* If we trace the story chronologically, we realise that Chapter Four, which encompasses Pangall's death, takes place in June (Midsummer Night is 24 June); Chapter Eight takes place the following year in Midsummer.

novel. Perspective constantly changes; we think we are seeing one thing when it turns out to be something entirely different. The violence of the sunlight in the opening paragraph is immediately contrasted with the chancellor hidden by shadow; but the incorporeal light becomes the 'most seeming solid thing'; it 'explod[es] in his face', it 'pile[s] into the open square', it 'smashe[s] through the rows of windows'. The sun-beams themselves, dancing with grains of dust, look for a moment as solid as the four pillars at the crossways; yet the four pillars themselves prove to be not what they seem when the iron probe grates and pierces 'in, through the stone skin . . . among the rubble with which the giants who had been on the earth in those days had filled the heart of the pil-lar' (Chapter Ten). When, later in Chapter One, Jocelin kneels to pray in the Lady Chapel and we are told 'Joy fell on the words like sunlight', we should remember how deceptive that sunlight may be.

Again, when the rain descends the perspective is changed: 'the bible in stone . . . [sinks] from glorification to homiletics'; the wind, like the sun, is portrayed as violent; it cuffs the air; it pushes Jocelin and strikes him 'like a blow'. The clouds hide the top of the cathedral so that he loses 'the sense of the size of it' (Chapter Three). In the December fog of Chapter Six the interior of the cathedral is often 'near enough pitch dark' but when Jocelin climbs into the tower he comes out into 'a blind-ing dazzle' of sunlight; yet, when he looks down on the surrounding countryside it is the fog which appears as 'a dazzling, burning patch over the valley and the city'; nothing else is visible.

So, the ever-changing weather of the seasons, the prismatic effect of sun through stained glass, the contrast of light and dark contribute to the tensions of the novel, reinforcing Jocelin's uncertainty and the reader's confusion, a confusion brought about not by accident but by deliberate design. This is a method used to powerful effect by Joseph Conrad (1857–1924), particularly in his brilliantly evocative short novel, *Heart of Darkness* (1902).

Another device which appears here and which Conrad also employed is the use of catch-phrases. 'Cost what you like' thinks Jocelin as he considers the spire during his quarrel with Anselm in Chapter Two. It is a phrase which he uses again and again as the cost, in human terms, mounts. Already in the first chapter we have learned that the financial burden of the spire is being borne by Jocelin's aunt Alison, who receives scant gratitude from her nephew himself; 'What is it? More money? Do you want two spires rather than one?' she enquires in her letter, but, as with all her earlier letters, Jocelin decrees that it shall remain unanswered.

Golding's style is often extremely complex. As a result of the mainly third-person narration through Jocelin's consciousness, the novel occasionally strays into the first person; sometimes this shift will be heralded by such words as 'he thought'; often there will be no such introduction as we move from his outside observation to the interior of his mind. Calligraphic devices such as bracketed interpolations and italics abound and punctuation is entirely individual as, for instance, in the following: 'Courage. Glory be. It is a final beginning.' (Chapter One) or the 'Heavy, pause, light, pause.' which indicates Jocelin's unsteady heartbeat in Chapter Eight.

At times we may feel that the novel is over-written and that unnecessary complications are introduced. When, for example, we are told that 'water ran out of [Jocelin's] eyes' we may wonder why he should not simply 'weep'. In another place* I have attempted to justify the use of a similar phrase in *The Inheritors*; here the usage seems less acceptable, though perhaps it is intended to suggest the involuntary nature of Jocelin's tears.

This brief consideration of Golding's use of language in *The Spire* is by no means exhaustive. The single most rewarding aspect of a study of Golding's work is to recognise the multi-layered pattern of his language which gives form and meaning to each separate novel and provides a link between all the novels.

* See *William Golding: The Inheritors* (York Notes series), 1983, p.42.

Part 4

Hints for study

NOTHING CAN BE A SUBSTITUTE for a thorough and careful reading of *The Spire* itself. Once it has been read, the story taken in and a general impression has been received, read it again, giving special attention to particular aspects of the novel. On your second reading take notes and jot down quotations; make sure that your note or quotation is followed by a bracketed page number (or chapter number if you are not using your own book and may have to use another edition on a subsequent reading). What kind of things will you be looking for as you study the novel more closely? You should consider at least some of the following:

1. narrative stance
2. point of view
3. setting
4. themes

5. source-works
6. characters
7. allegorical aspects
8. language

Try to think of other interesting or significant aspects of the novel which you could add to this list. (Part 3 of these Notes may help you.)

Always remember to return to the text in order to support or illustrate points you are making. Critics may suggest ideas to you but you should ensure that you accept these ideas only if your own knowledge of the novel confirms them. A critic can be wrong; or two critics may disagree. Even if you believe a critic to be right, check that the text is able to support his argument. Try to find quotations other than those he has used which could have been used on his side; are there other passages in the novel which appear to refute his arguments? When you were reading Part 3 of these Notes did you agree with everything that was said? If so, did you try to think of other quotations that supported what was said? If you disagreed, are you able to illustrate your own beliefs with quotations from the text?

Before you can think in any detail about a novel you must be well acquainted with what happens in it. This novel is particularly difficult in some ways because so much of the 'story' is elusive, deduced rather than explicitly stated. As a start, try to answer the following simple questions without looking at your copy of *The Spire*:

1. Which four characters represent the four pillars at the crossways?
2. Who is Gilbert?

3. How high is the spire when it is finished?
4. Why is the building of the spire such a problem?
5. Who is Father Adam?
6. What does Jocelin call him, and why?
7. How did the friendship between Jocelin and Father Anselm begin?
8. What offices in the Church does each of them hold?
9. What is the name of Jocelin's aunt? and why does Jocelin despise her?
10. Why does Jocelin visit Roger Mason not long before his death?
11. Who is with Jocelin when he dies?

Check your answers by going back to the book. Which chapter gives you the correct answer to question 8? to question 10? If you were unable to give correct answers to all these simple questions you do not know the book well enough and you should read it again. If you answered all the questions correctly you are ready to move on to a fuller discussion of the novel.

In the first chapter of his book a novelist has two major tasks: first, he must lay down the foundations for the rest of what he has to say, whether it be through careful attention to setting, delineation of character or preparation for the plot; secondly, he must grip the attention of his readers so that they want to go on reading. Look again at Chapter One of *The Spire*; it starts with the word 'He', referring to Jocelin, but the first paragraph is as much about the cathedral setting as about the Dean. It is a worthwhile exercise to identify passages which show how Golding establishes the setting.

By the end of this first chapter an attentive reader has a very good picture of the cathedral and the disruption it is suffering – but notice how indirect the descriptions are. Golding does not deliberately paint in his setting; we piece it together incidentally as the novel proceeds and it is integral with the characters and the plot.

Most of the principal characters appear, or are at least named, in this first chapter: Jocelin, Goody Pangall, Father Anselm, Gilbert the dumb man, Pangall, Father Adam and Jocelin's Aunt Alison. Find a few quotations that tell us, even at this early stage, something about two or three of these. Which major characters have not yet appeared? Since you should have already read the whole of the novel, find some further quotations to show how Golding has prepared us for the plot. Does the first chapter persuade us to go on reading? If so, by what means? If not, why not?

By now you should have gathered enough material to be able to answer the question 'Show how Golding prepares us in the first chapter for what is to follow.' Try to write such an essay; before you write it you should put your ideas in some sort of order and make a plan. For instance:

(a) *Cathedral setting:* physical aspects (model); light through stained-glass windows; effects of building work on building itself and upon Church life; officers of cathedral.

(b) *Characters:* Jocelin established as main character and main consciousness; his satellites – the dumb man, Father Adam and perhaps Goody Pangall; his problems – Pangall the caretaker and Aunt Alison.

(c) *Plot:* building of the spire; suggestion of intrigue concerned with finance for building; introduction of female protagonist, Goody Pangall.

(d) *Underlying themes:* Jocelin's angel (disease and idea of good and evil); suggestion of dissension; sex. Golding's language suggests these underlying themes; note how allegorical aspects of the novel are prepared for here.

Now write the essay!

A good way of getting to know a novel well is by examining a particular incident and seeing how it bears on theme, plot, character and other aspects of the book. In examining one incident you are forced to examine a number of other incidents as well. We could take as our example here the incident in Chapter Six when Jocelin climbs the tower and discovers that Roger Mason and Goody Pangall are together in the swallow's nest. Apart from throwing light on Jocelin's character and confirming our knowledge of the illicit relationship between Goody and Roger, this refers us to various other episodes in the book. Examine the two pages from the paragraph beginning 'Then, one day, Jocelin . . .' to 'The cost of building material.' Try to make connections with other parts of the novel: for instance, 'the news of the extra expense' of the spire should remind us of where the money for the building originates (see Chapters One and Ten); this, in turn, brings to mind the sinful liaison between Alison and the King and prepares us for Jocelin's discovery of Goody's and Roger's adultery. What connections can you make with the following ideas and images from this extract?

(a) 'he would have to affix his own private seal to these documents'
(b) 'his angel was at once a blessing and a great wearisomeness to him'
(c) 'red hair'
(d) 'a wolf-howl'
(e) 'some trapped animal'
(f) 'I didn't laugh – did I?'

(*g*) 'a green girl running in the close . . . the shy smile and the singing of the child's game'
(*h*) 'the tent'
(*i*) 'the arranged marriage with the lame man'
(*j*) 'The cost of building material'.

Each of these quotations has its origin in, or leads to, one or more other incidents in the novel. Try to find them. Put your information in some sort of order, showing what you have learned about Jocelin, Roger and Goody, about the plot, about the underlying themes and meanings of the novel. Now you should be able to write a second essay, discussing the significance of this episode in the novel as a whole.

This final section has been designed, not to save you from working, but to help you to work more efficiently. For this reason you have been constantly urged in these Notes to find things out for yourself, to become well acquainted with Golding's text and to return to it again and again. Ways of dealing with various questions have been suggested and you have been asked to return to the novel to collect your material. Here are more questions to answer followed by model answers to two of them:

1. Consider the significance of the title *The Spire* for this novel.
2. Consider the advantages and disadvantages of presenting the story through Jocelin's consciousness.
3. Retell in the first person, from Roger Mason's point of view, the discussion in Chapter Four between Roger and Jocelin in which Jocelin traps the master builder.
4. Consider the significance of the part played in the novel by *either* (*a*) Father Adam *or* (*b*) Aunt Alison *or* (*c*) Gilbert the dumb man.
5. Write a character sketch of *one* of the following: (*a*) Jocelin; (*b*) Anselm; (*c*) Roger Mason.
6. How does Golding prepare us for the sexual aspects of the novel?
7. Consider the theme of Evil in *The Spire*.
8. Discuss the allegorical aspects of *The Spire*.
9. Recommend this novel to a friend, giving substantial reasons why you think he/she should read it.
10. Using the novel as your material, write a section for an historical guidebook describing the cathedral.

Model answers

The model answers which follow are the result of considerable preparation. Before an essay is started and after an initial thorough reading, the text must be skimmed through, notes taken and quotations jotted down. Then an essay plan must be made. Only after that is it possible to write a rough draft of the essay. What appears here is a more polished piece of work. Once you have read the essays try to work out the original plan for them.

---

1. Consider the significance of the title *The Spire* for this novel.

Golding once said that he had thought of calling this novel 'An Erection in Barchester', Barchester being the name for Salisbury which Trollope used in his novels. This remark helps to underline the allegorical significance of the actual title, though *The Spire* is both more elegant and more subtle.

The novel takes as its overt theme the building of a cathedral spire and the background setting is loosely based on medieval Salisbury. Golding's town and cathedral, however, remain unnamed and the emphasis is not on the great church which, at the opening of the novel, has already been used for worship for a hundred and fifty years but on the building work being undertaken to erect the spire. The foundations of the original cathedral are shallow and below them is marshy land. Thus, our initial interest in the novel centres on whether it is physically possible for the spire to be built and whether, once completed, it will fall in the first winter storm. As the work climbs higher and higher a constant physical tension is sustained through the ringing and singing of the stones, through the bending of the pillars at the crossways, through the leaning of the spire and through the final terrible discovery that the pillars are not solid but merely shells filled with rubble. Our attention, however, like Jocelin's, is always on the spire. Even in the last three chapters when the building is finished and the Holy Nail hammered home, the physical presence of the spire pervades the narration; it is Jocelin's 'prayer in stone', his 'spire of prayer'; it is the last thing he sees – something dividing the blue sky through the window of his death chamber, 'still and silent, but rushing upwards to some point at the sky's end' (Chapter Twelve).

The spire is also a phallic symbol representing the sexual side of man. Jocelin, without understanding its significance, introduces this idea in the first chapter when he considers the model of the cathedral; he compares it to a 'man lying on his back' and sees the spire 'springing, projecting, bursting, erupting from the heart of the building'. The fulfilment of his religious vision becomes a kind of vicarious fulfilment of his sexual desire, the final consummation of both spires occurring in Chapter Nine.

The Spire therefore appears to be a very apt title for this novel: it suggests the subject of the plot and at the same time it refers delicately to one of the principal underlying themes.

4 (b). Consider the significance of the part played in the novel by Aunt Alison.

Alison appears in the novel only once, in Chapter Ten. She is, however, introduced to the reader in the first chapter through a letter (one of a series of such missives) she has sent to Jocelin.

We know little about Alison herself. She is Jocelin's aunt, his mother's sister, the 'naughty one' as she comments in Chapter Ten, who became a rich woman through being mistress to the King. The King's death has frustrated the fulfilment of his promise to her that she should be buried 'in Winchester, among the kings' (Chapter One) but she clings to the hope of a tomb in the cathedral where her nephew is Dean.

Her letter is one of the early pointers to the discord and rottenness at the heart of Jocelin's belief, for it shows him in an unfavourable light. The letter is an appeal for forgiveness and understanding; Alison knows she has done wrong in God's eyes and Jocelin's but that is all past and she is ready to pay for forgiveness (a practice not unknown in the medieval Church). She has indeed already given Jocelin money to build the spire and he has embraced the gift but not the giver; he despises her and refuses to answer her letters, though he nevertheless accepts the tainted present; as she says, 'It was a different and a much quicker answer you gave when the question was one of money' (Chapter One).

As the novel proceeds we see that Jocelin himself is little better than his aunt. He lusts after the child who later becomes Goody Pangall and, in order to quieten his lust, he denies her her womanhood by marrying her to the lame and impotent Pangall. Even Goody, the object of his desire, has feet of clay, for her adultery with Roger Mason puts her on a par with Alison herself. Yet when Jocelin finally confesses his lecherous thoughts to his aunt she is horrified and shuns him; even she cannot accept prurience in God's minister. Thus we see how the evil in Alison's life is reflected in the lives of others and that Jocelin's condemnation of her hides a subconscious hypocrisy.

Equally significant to an understanding of the novel is the revelation finally made by Alison in Chapter Ten and confirmed by Father Anselm in the following chapter: Jocelin had believed in his vocation, believed that he had been chosen and given responsibility in the Church because God had singled him out. From his aunt he learns that preferment came to him, not because of his own merit, but through her liaison with the King. Thus he realises that his whole life has been a sham, that all his achievements, his rise in the Church, the spire itself, have been built upon the prostitution of his aunt.

Though she appears to have only a minor part, the role of Aunt Alison is perhaps, together with that of Jocelin, the most significant one in the novel.

Part 5

Suggestions for further reading

The text

The best text is that published by Faber & Faber, London, 1964 and available in paperback since 1965.

Other novels by William Golding

Golding's novels often throw light on each other and it will be useful to read:

Lord of the Flies, Faber & Faber, London, 1954.
The Inheritors, Faber & Faber, London, 1955.
Pincher Martin, Faber & Faber, London, 1956.

William Golding's life

There is so far no biography of William Golding. He has himself, however, published two books of essays which contain a certain amount of autobiographical information:

The Hot Gates and Other Occasional Pieces, Faber & Faber, London, 1965.
A Moving Target, Faber & Faber, London, 1982.

Critical studies

Whilst an enormous amount of critical attention has been paid to *Lord of the Flies* nothing very substantial has been published exclusively on *The Spire*. There are useful sections or chapters, however, in the following:

HYNES, SAMUEL: *William Golding* (Columbia Essays on Modern Writers 2) Columbia University Press, New York and London, 1968.
KINKEAD-WEEKES, M. and GREGOR, I.: *William Golding: A Critical Study*, Faber & Faber, London, 1967.
OLDSEY, B.S. and WEINTRAUB, S.: *The Art of William Golding*,

Harcourt, Brace & World, New York, 1968. This book is particularly helpful on sources for *The Spire*.

TIGER, VIRGINIA: *William Golding: The Dark Fields of Discovery*, Calder & Boyars, London, 1974. A lively and very readable book.

Other books referred to in the text

AA Hand-picked Tours in Britain, Drive Publications, Basingstoke, 1977.

CONRAD, JOSEPH: *Heart of Darkness* (1902); published in Everyman's Library, Dent, London, 1974.

Salisbury Cathedral, Pitkin Pictorial Guides and Souvenir Books, Pitkin Pictorials, London, n.d.

SPEAR, HILDA D.: *William Golding: The Inheritors* (York Notes series), Longman/York Press, London, 1983.

The author of these notes

HILDA D. SPEAR was educated at Furzedown College of Education, London, the University of London, and the University of Leicester. She has taught in various schools, colleges of education and universities, including Purdue University, Indiana. She is now a Senior Lecturer in the Department of English, the University of Dundee. Her publications include an annotated edition of *The English Poems of C.S. Calverley* (1974); *The Poems and Selected Letters of Charles Hamilton Sorley* (1978) and *Remembering, We Forget* (1979). She wrote the biographical and bibliographical section of *The Pelican Guide to English Literature V*, and she has published articles on teaching English as well as on nineteenth- and twentieth-century writers. She is also the author of York Notes on *The Mayor of Casterbridge* by Thomas Hardy, *The Rainbow* by D.H. Lawrence, *Youth* and *Typhoon* by Joseph Conrad and *The Inheritors* by William Golding.

The first 250 titles

CHINUA ACHEBE
A Man of the People
Arrow of God
Things Fall Apart

ELECHI AMADI
The Concubine

ANONYMOUS
Beowulf

JOHN ARDEN
Serjeant Musgrave's Dance

AYI KWEI ARMAH
The Beautyful Ones Are Not Yet Born

JANE AUSTEN
Emma
Mansfield Park
Northanger Abbey
Persuasion
Pride and Prejudice
Sense and Sensibility

HONORÉ DE BALZAC
Le Père Goriot

SAMUEL BECKETT
Waiting for Godot

SAUL BELLOW
Henderson, The Rain King

ARNOLD BENNETT
Anna of the Five Towns

WILLIAM BLAKE
Songs of Innocence, Songs of Experience

ROBERT BOLT
A Man For All Seasons

ANNE BRONTË
The Tenant of Wildfell Hall

CHARLOTTE BRONTË
Jane Eyre

EMILY BRONTË
Wuthering Heights

ROBERT BROWNING
Men and Women

JOHN BUCHAN
The Thirty-Nine Steps

JOHN BUNYAN
The Pilgrim's Progress

GEORGE GORDON, LORD BYRON
Selected Poems

ALBERT CAMUS
L'Etranger (The Outsider)

GEOFFREY CHAUCER
Prologue to the Canterbury Tales
The Franklin's Tale
The Knight's Tale
The Merchant's Tale
The Miller's Tale
The Nun's Priest's Tale
The Pardoner's Tale
The Wife of Bath's Tale
Troilus and Criseyde

ANTON CHEKHOV
The Cherry Orchard

SAMUEL TAYLOR COLERIDGE
Selected Poems

WILKIE COLLINS
The Moonstone
The Woman in White

SIR ARTHUR CONAN DOYLE
The Hound of the Baskervilles

WILLIAM CONGREVE
The Way of the World

JOSEPH CONRAD
Heart of Darkness
Lord Jim
Nostromo
The Secret Agent
Youth and *Typhoon*

BRUCE DAWE
Selected Poems

DANIEL DEFOE
A Journal of the Plague Year
Moll Flanders
Robinson Crusoe

CHARLES DICKENS
A Tale of Two Cities
Bleak House
David Copperfield
Great Expectations
Hard Times
Little Dorrit
Nicholas Nickleby
Oliver Twist
Our Mutual Friend
The Pickwick Papers

EMILY DICKINSON
Selected Poems

JOHN DONNE
Selected Poems

THEODORE DREISER
Sister Carrie

GEORGE ELIOT
Adam Bede
Silas Marner
The Mill on the Floss

T. S. ELIOT
Four Quartets
Murder in the Cathedral
Selected Poems
The Waste Land

GEORGE FARQUHAR
The Beaux Stratagem

WILLIAM FAULKNER
Absalom, Absalom!
As I Lay Dying
Go Down, Moses
The Sound and the Fury

HENRY FIELDING
Joseph Andrews
Tom Jones

F. SCOTT FITZGERALD
Tender is the Night
The Great Gatsby

E. M. FORSTER
A Passage to India
Howards End

ATHOL FUGARD
Selected Plays

JOHN GALSWORTHY
Strife

MRS GASKELL
North and South

WILLIAM GOLDING
Lord of the Flies
The Inheritors

OLIVER GOLDSMITH
She Stoops to Conquer
The Vicar of Wakefield

ROBERT GRAVES
Goodbye to All That

GRAHAM GREENE
Brighton Rock
The Power and the Glory

THOMAS HARDY
Far from the Madding Crowd
Jude the Obscure
Selected Poems
Tess of the D'Urbervilles
The Mayor of Casterbridge
The Return of the Native
The Trumpet Major
The Woodlanders
Under the Greenwood Tree

L. P. HARTLEY
The Go-Between
The Shrimp and the Anemone

NATHANIEL HAWTHORNE
The Scarlet Letter

ERNEST HEMINGWAY
A Farewell to Arms
For Whom the Bell Tolls
The African Stories
The Old Man and the Sea

GEORGE HERBERT
Selected Poems

HERMANN HESSE
Steppenwolf

BARRY HINES
Kes

ANTHONY HOPE
The Prisoner of Zenda

GERARD MANLEY HOPKINS
Selected Poems

WILLIAM DEAN HOWELLS
The Rise of Silas Lapham

RICHARD HUGHES
A High Wind in Jamaica

THOMAS HUGHES
Tom Brown's Schooldays

ALDOUS HUXLEY
Brave New World

HENRIK IBSEN
A Doll's House
Ghosts
Hedda Gabler

HENRY JAMES
Daisy Miller
The Europeans
The Portrait of a Lady
The Turn of the Screw
Washington Square

SAMUEL JOHNSON
Rasselas

BEN JONSON
The Alchemist
Volpone

JAMES JOYCE
Dubliners

JOHN KEATS
Selected Poems

RUDYARD KIPLING
Kim

D. H. LAWRENCE
Sons and Lovers
The Rainbow
Women in Love

CAMARA LAYE
L'Enfant Noir

HARPER LEE
To Kill a Mocking-Bird

LAURIE LEE
Cider with Rosie

THOMAS MANN
Tonio Kröger

CHRISTOPHER MARLOWE
Doctor Faustus
Edward II

ANDREW MARVELL
Selected Poems

W. SOMERSET MAUGHAM
Of Human Bondage
Selected Short Stories

J. MEADE FALKNER
Moonfleet

HERMAN MELVILLE
Billy Budd
Moby Dick

THOMAS MIDDLETON
Women Beware Women

THOMAS MIDDLETON and WILLIAM ROWLEY
The Changeling

ARTHUR MILLER
Death of a Salesman
The Crucible

JOHN MILTON
Paradise Lost I & II
Paradise Lost IV & IX
Selected Poems

V. S. NAIPAUL
A House for Mr Biswas

SEAN O'CASEY
Juno and the Paycock
The Shadow of a Gunman

GABRIEL OKARA
The Voice

EUGENE O'NEILL
Mourning Becomes Electra

GEORGE ORWELL
Animal Farm
Nineteen Eighty-four

The first eleven titles

YORK HANDBOOKS form a companion series to York Notes and are designed to meet the wider needs of students of English and related fields. Each volume is a compact study of a given subject area, written by an authority with experience in communicating the essential ideas to students of all levels.

AN INTRODUCTORY GUIDE TO ENGLISH LITERATURE
by MARTIN STEPHEN

PREPARING FOR EXAMINATIONS IN ENGLISH LITERATURE
by NEIL McEWAN

AN INTRODUCTION TO LITERARY CRITICISM
by RICHARD DUTTON

THE ENGLISH NOVEL
by IAN MILLIGAN

ENGLISH POETRY
by CLIVE T. PROBYN

STUDYING CHAUCER
by ELISABETH BREWER

STUDYING SHAKESPEARE
by MARTIN STEPHEN *and* PHILIP FRANKS

AN ABC OF SHAKESPEARE
His Plays, Theatre, Life and Times
by P.C. Bayley

ENGLISH USAGE
by COLIN G. HEY

A DICTIONARY OF LITERARY TERMS
by MARTIN GRAY

READING THE SCREEN
An Introduction to Film Studies
by JOHN IZOD